E NCE OF PLACE

M rchitecture

ELEENA JAMIL

Foreword
Dean Hawkes

Contents

Foreword

"EVERY COUNTRY BUILDS its houses in response to its climate. At this moment of general diffusion, of international scientific techniques, I propose only one house for all countries, the house of exact breathing."[1]

These words were spoken by Le Corbusier in a lecture he gave in Buenos Aires in 1929.

They foretell the profound transformation of architecture's relationship to climate that was to take place in the 20th century, when the historic method of using the form and material of a building to respond to climate was replaced by mechanical systems of heating, cooling, ventilation and lighting. From that moment, "one house for all climates" became the dominant strategy across the diverse climate systems of the planet, in buildings for all purposes. The most familiar manifestation of this is the glass skyscraper, which, with its sealed envelope and air-conditioning systems, dominates the skyline of every major city of the globe. This may be regarded as a logical outcome of technological "progress" and as having little or no cultural consequence, but that would be to disregard the evidence that architecture is fundamentally a cultural and social enterprise, and that the relationship between a building and the climate in which it is set is one of the key determinants of its cultural and social value.

It is almost a century since Le Corbusier made his prophetic statement and he could not have anticipated that, by the beginning of the 21st century, environmental design in architecture would be changed beyond all precedent by the pressures of human-influenced climate change. As global temperatures rise and extreme weather events become almost commonplace, the assumptions and conventions by which buildings have been designed in relation to climate face significant challenges. Human influence on climate has many sources, but a key element comes from the energy-consuming systems without which the majority of modern buildings would not function. Buildings are now part of the problem.

In contrast to this tendency, a powerful alternative has emerged and gained support in the last half a century or so. One of the major contributions to this came from Victor Olgyay, who in his teaching at Princeton University and in his seminal book, *Design with Climate*, showed that design *with* rather than *against* climate was credible in the modern era.[2] Further support for this position came from Kenneth Frampton who, in making the case for a "Critical Regionalism", wrote that architecture "may find its governing inspiration in such things as the range and quality of the local light, or in a tectonic derived from a peculiar structural mode, or in the topography of a given site".[3]

Together, Olgyay, Frampton and others have made the case for architecture of our day to return to and reinterpret the historic method of shaping environments in response to place, climate and culture, as well as to address human need and the increasingly urgent issue of our planet's climate.

This is the background against which Eleena Jamil has practised architecture for almost a quarter of a century, following ten years during which she studied and worked in the UK. On her return to Kuala Lumpur the city was at the forefront of the global tendency in architecture, symbolised, above all, by the twin, air-conditioned structures of the Petronas Towers. In contrast to, or, one might equally say, in opposition to this, she has pursued an architecture that reconsiders the environmental strategy of buildings based on the climate-responsive paradigms of Olgyay, Frampton and others. In Kuala Lumpur, at latitude 3.1°N, the sun's daily passage across the zenith of the sky and the almost-unvarying diurnal and seasonal temperatures, averaging close to 30°C, both define the climate and make it challenging, but may also provide inspiration for architects. Taking careful notice of the material, form and detail of vernacular buildings of the region, Jamil has explored multiple new architectural possibilities in the service of the inhabitants of the 21st-century city.

In a sequence of projects, she has investigated the potential of indigenous materials, such as bamboo and meranti, to shape enclosures finely attuned to the local climate. For example, the Shadow Garden Pavilion, in the grounds of an art gallery, is a study in translating the daily passage of the sun into architectural form, and anticipates, in principle if not in scale, the much larger Bamboo Playhouse in the Perdana Botanical Gardens. Here, a network of interlinked bamboo canopies hovers above a stepped platform to create a microclimate of shady and breezy places at the heart of the gardens. The same material is adopted in the construction of the prototype Bamboo Classroom built in 2010 on the Bicol Peninsula in the Philippines. The plan and section of the building follow the familiar typology of the linear classroom block, but invest this with new utility and meaning through the delicacy and elegance of the material.

A key element of Jamil's work when designing more conventional projects – schools, houses and other urban buildings – has been to refer to typology. She writes about the "inherent order in existing built forms as fundamental to our practice's climatic response in architecture". The power of this proposition is demonstrated by the Desa Mahkota School, where the forms and principles of the traditional Malay house are reinterpreted and extended in scale to become an elegant and environmentally appropriate setting for 1,200 pupils. The idea of the "outdoor room" in Malay culture and architecture is expressed in elegant designs for single family houses, Vermani House (2014), Wangsa House (2019) and End-lot House (2020). All are demonstrably of their time and accommodate 21st-century expectations, but also revive deep regional traditions and practices. At a larger scale, the Buzz.ar (2019) is a community building at the heart of a new neighbourhood on the outskirts of Kuala Lumpur. This returns to the idea of shading that was key to the Bamboo Playhouse project, but now presented as an elegant, folded canopy of modern materials for sheltering social gatherings, children's play and small commercial enterprises. Shading is also the key ingredient of the Karwa Mosque in Penang (2020), but here takes the form of an elegant mihrab screen of perforated concrete panels that encloses and shelters a courtyard terrace from which the building is entered. Once again, a tradition is transformed.

In architecture, the relationship between theory and practice is complex, but the best validation of any theoretical proposition lies in its translation into practice, when the abstractions of theory become expressed as form. In this book Eleena Jamil presents an exemplary account of how, over two decades, her practice has pursued this objective in creating an architecture that is precisely attuned to the climate, culture and traditions of its location.

Dean Hawkes
Cambridge
October 2023

ENDNOTES

1 Reproduced in Le Corbusier, *Precisions on the Present State of Architecture and City Planning*, Paris: Crés et Cie, 1930, Cambridge, MA: MIT Press, 1991.

2 Olgyay, Victor, *Design with Climate: Bioclimatic Approach to Architectural Regionalism*, Princeton: Princeton University Press, 1984.

3 Frampton, Kenneth, "Towards a Critical Regionalism: Six Points for an Architecture of Resistance", in Hal Foster ed, *Postmodern Culture*, London and Concord, MA: Pluto Press, 1983.

Grounding Architecture

Architecture does not travel well, and, when it does, it loses its connection to specific places, materials, and history. Without even realising it, the past is wiped out, creating universal architectural solutions to what was never a universal problem. In the 20th century, as the result of international industrialisation, places slowly ceased to be distinct and became anonymous nonentities. This phenomenon occurred in numerous developing cities, accelerated by aggressive investment strategies and corporate construction methods. Any rejection of this tendency is seen as pursuing provincial attitudes and failing to embrace contemporaneity.

Kuala Lumpur started growing rapidly when it vigorously embraced "newness", which it continues to do today. Nonetheless, for me, returning to practise in the city in 2000, after more than a decade of studying and working in the UK, was exciting. Malaysia was one of the most urbanised nations in South East Asia, its capital city was booming, and marking its economic success was the tallest building in the world at the time, the Petronas Twin Towers. Today, the city continues to grow rapidly, with the old fabric razed to make way for new energy-hungry, air-conditioned conurbations, driven by a combination of historical colonialism, booming economic development following independence in the late 1950s, and population movement from rural areas to urban centres. Success stories often take the form of glass towers glistening in the intense equatorial sun, with heavy elevated highways snaking between them. The city has become one of the cool kids on the block.

Against the backdrop of this fast-developing metropolis and its hinterland, questions about what is appropriate have been explored through my practice's early competition schemes and later built work. In common with many parts of the developing world, Malaysia has an architectural tradition both in terms of materials and craftsmanship, which is on the verge of disappearing as industrialisation and modernisation take over. The period of study and studio work I spent abroad provided a fresh perspective when examining these very familiar aspects and the qualities that constitute their identity. I find the relationship between form and making, and the use of local architectural traditions far more interesting than questions of style and ornamentation. The simple patterns, rhythms and orientations that emerge from the construction process, and how people use spaces and go about their daily lives within the built environment, are much more significant for developing place-specific architectural solutions.

The connection between geography and architecture was instilled in me by my studies at the Welsh School of Architecture, under the tutelage of Professors Dean Hawkes, Phil Jones and Wayne Forster. The school emphasised the significance of local geography and climate on the shape and form of the built environment. Though it may seem a cliché to mention it, in the 1990s and 2000s, climate-responsive shape and form were often ignored in the rush to urbanise developing countries. This phenomenon was, and still is, encouraged by fossil-fuel-driven energy and technological advances, which suppress nature in the interests of providing comfortable indoor conditions.

A visit to Helsinki, made possible through a T Alwyn Lloyd Memorial Travelling Scholarship at the end of my third year at the Welsh School, in the

Opposite
Kuala Lumpur City

late summer of 1994, opened my eyes to Alvar Aalto and the intimate connection he forged between his architecture and the Finnish landscape. Standing in the house and studio he and Aino, his wife at the time, built in the quiet residential neighbourhood of Munkkiniemi, in Helsinki, I was interested in how they designed their living spaces. Here, modernist spaces with a typically functionalist approach – free-flowing, open, bright, and practical – combined with elements that reinforced a more complex relationship with natural conditions. Both house and studio look unassuming from the street and feature an L-shaped volume wrapped around a garden, or, in the case of the studio, an outdoor amphitheatre, and the main living and working spaces in both buildings relate directly to the outdoors through carefully placed openings. The wood used in both the interiors and exteriors, often in vertical striations, echoes the tall, skinny trees of the Nordic boreal forest, and contrasts with the horizontality of the painted brickwork walls. Sensitively placed openings, either in a horizontal pictorial format at low levels, or as vertical soaring shafts at high ones, bathe the interior with daylight, allowing the rich materials and living plants to display their changing tones and textures as the sun moves around them. This interplay of inside/outside, vertical/horizontal, and natural/manmade materials creates an architecture that reflects the particularities of its surroundings.

Sugden House, in Hertfordshire, UK, which I explored as part of my PhD thesis titled *Rethinking Modernism: The Sugden House and The Mother's House*, made me aware of how to achieve a direct and realistic response to existing contexts. Designed by Alison and Peter Smithson in 1955–56, the house, at first glance, looks ordinary. It uses standard materials from the building merchant's yard: second-hand stock bricks, Marley concrete tiles and standard Z-framed galvanised steel sashes. However, its apparent ordinariness and powerful inelegance belie its curious character. The windows are larger than normal and L-shaped, which are not typically used in the area, earning the house the nickname "window home" among locals. And the steep pitch of the roof towards the back of the house, with its tight eaves and appearance of coalescing with the rough brickwork of the external walls, is entirely disproportionate to the front. In August 2020, I spent an afternoon at the house with its owners, Derek and Jean Sugden, together with my research supervisor, Professor Dean Hawkes, and had the opportunity to examine it closely. Internally, the rooms' shapes, sizes and openings correspond closely to their purposes, with each having its own *raison d'être*. In this respect, the house embodies a return to fundamentals and a way of building without style and rhetoric as a direct response to need and context, coupled with wit and dexterity.

I returned to Malaysia enriched by a new sensitivity to the local surroundings, and with the realisation that modern architecture can evolve in surprising ways when it encounters different cultural and climatic conditions from those in which it first developed. The reciprocity of modernisation and industrialisation with the unique conditions of a place means that regional and local architecture can contribute to a wider architectural discourse.

Many of the vernacular buildings in Malaysia and South East Asia are the result of a response to climate that roots buildings in local construction techniques and natural material culture. The earliest building form – a simple shelter made from local natural materials such as bamboo, timber and palm leaves, with a floor raised on stilts to keep it dry, and four columns holding up a steeply pitched roof with low overhangs to expel rainwater and protect the interior from direct sun – evolved into the traditional Malay house, or *kampung* house, a sophisticated building typology that sits on the earth lightly. The space below the house is used for work such as weaving, sewing, or repairing boats,

1 Alvar Aalto Studio
2 Sugden House

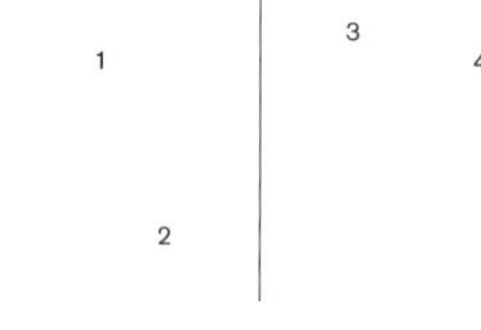

1 Malay kampung house
2 Devoid of furniture, most daily life activities take place directly on the floor in a Malay kampung house
3 Colonial building in Kuala Lumpur
4 Chinese shophouse in Malacca

and there is usually a veranda where one can sit comfortably and receive guests. Internally, living quarters are open-plan with apertures at low and high levels to encourage cross-ventilation.

Local colonial and post-colonial architecture in Malaysia displays similar responses to the climate, with structures made from modern materials such as brick, concrete and plaster, but also characterised by solar shading devices, external perforated skins, and colonnaded verandas on the perimeter that impart a sense of grandeur. These features were all necessary to shade spaces and moderate indoor temperatures before air-conditioning became the cheap and standard solution. New towns that mushroomed in the early 20th century across the country contained high streets lined with Chinese merchants' shophouses, which featured multiple courtyards surrounded by louvred and decorative perforated screens as a way of introducing light and air into their deep linear volumes. Along the street, the ground floor was set back from the upper levels to provide a public footpath – popularly known as the five-foot walkway – and shelter it from the elements.

Human responses to these local conditions and places, and the way people use and react to them, are recognised as unique to this region of the world. There is a sense of ambiguity in the domestic living spaces of traditional South East Asian architecture, with little in the way of furniture to denote function and use, so most activities take place directly on the floor. Instead, use is indicated through a hierarchical arrangement of spaces, from the public veranda to the private inner sanctum of the house, which permits gender separation, and from the biggest and, usually, tallest space, to the smallest and lowest such as the kitchen. This functional adumbration also permits flexibility: spaces are transformed easily, enabling different activities during occasions such as religious festivities and celebrations of weddings or births.

The complex richness of Malaysia's architectural tradition arose from a need to maximise minimal resources, resulting in modest structures that communicate a sense of continuity between past and present. Some of my favourite typologies are the simple, banal developments that form part of everyday life, such as the bustling wet markets dotted around Malaysian urban neighbourhoods, which sell fresh produce in open, light-filled, well-ventilated and highly adapted structures. Also dispersed along road networks are the "R&R" services, as they are popularly known, designed around multiple landscaped courtyards, which contain food courts, bathrooms, prayer rooms and children's play areas, separated by little green patches and connected by covered walkways. Another typology is schools, which are among the most interesting low-energy buildings in Malaysia. Many schools use passive strategies to keep them cool during the day rather than mechanised systems, including natural ventilation and classrooms arranged in narrow linear blocks with openings at high and low levels, connected by generous, shaded corridors.

DIALOGUE WITH PLACE

In a keynote lecture presented at the 12th International Docomomo Conference in Espoo, Finland, in August 2012, renowned Finnish architect Juhani Pallasmaa, spoke of the importance of buildings being rooted in the historicity of their place, and of contributing to a sense of cultural continuum:

1 R&R services
2 Typical school

"The first responsibility of the architect is always to the inherited landscape or urban setting; a profound building has to enhance its wider context and give it new meanings and aesthetic qualities. Responsible architecture improves the landscape of its location and gives its lesser architectural neighbours new qualities instead of degrading them. It always enters a dialogue with existent conditions; profound buildings are not self-centred monologues."[1]

As described in the following chapters, the modest projects produced by my studio demonstrate an architectural approach that aims to respect the continuity of past, present, and place. Our work avoids both nostalgia of the past and the recreation of a formal vernacular language. Instead, culture is seen as the product of a collective and non-conscious system that has evolved over generations and that maintains a sense of history, context, coherence and hierarchy within a technological and social environment that is constantly changing.

The repeated use of bamboo, timber and other local materials, along with low-tech and traditional building techniques, aims to connect our designs to the land and to its inherited crafts and craftspeople. The dwindling of these resources in modern construction, as materials such as steel, glass, plastic and concrete have taken over, has caused a gradual loss of historicity and identity in the urban fabric. Their reintroduction will demand extensive experimentation and convincing clients and authorities of their viability in modern construction, in a way that sustains energy sustainability and community values.

An archetypal image of Malaysia's geography is of lush rainforest flourishing in the high temperatures and humidity. Sunshine is continuous for most of the year, with little filtering from clouds or vapours except in the forest, where the floor is kept cool by the huge tree canopy. In clearings and built areas, relief from the heat is provided by the seasonal monsoon rain, which can last for weeks at a time and enables trees and plants to thrive. Blessed with such unique natural characteristics, we have resolved to pursue strategies of inclusion rather than exclusion. In our spaces, large overhangs and shading devices cut down sunlight to prevent overheating, but it is not completely excluded. Carefully placed openings permit the sun to penetrate in the mornings when the weather is cool, while "outdoor rooms", such as tree- and plant-filled courtyards and terraces, allow internal spaces to blend with their natural surroundings.

My understanding of place in the context of my practice and how it can shape architecture is not always clear-cut. A place contains not only physical data (geography, topography, climate, people, and materials) but also aspects of memory relating to tradition, culture, and history. These may take the form of the "present absences" of a place, which are inherent in its identity. However, all aspects of a place can only be truly understood through physical experience, which is missing when viewed through photographs, moving images, or technologies such as Google Earth. Wherever an architect works, they need hands that see and eyes that feel, to construct a contemporary fabric of identity woven from details of time and place.

ENDNOTE

1 Pallasmaa, Juhani, "Newness, Tradition and Identity — Existential Meaning in Architecture", keynote lecture presented at the 12th International Docomomo Conference in Espoo, Finland, 2012.

About Making

The origins of the architecture profession lie in the craft of making. Before it was considered a profession, architecture was practised in close association with a building's physical construction on-site. For example, in South East Asia, the making of a traditional Malay house was carried out without drawings and was considered a manual occupation. A sophisticated form of rural domestic architecture, the Malay house consisted of modular rectangular volumes raised on stilts and was built by the traditional *tukang* or craftsperson, who acted as both architect and maker, assisted by a team of apprentices and local community members. Practising a highly ordered building process that reflected a set of rituals and local beliefs, and using anthropometric proportions, the *tukang* was well versed in the interlocking timber-jointing technique known as *tanggam*. They would also have had a deep knowledge of the local environment and natural building materials, including timber, rattan and thatch, and known where and how to source them. In addition to these skills, they were a master carver who produced intricate ornamental carvings and understood their aesthetic principles and meanings.

For the *tukang*, ideas, forms and their execution were perceived as a single organic process. Like many other craftspeople, they picked up their craft through rigorous apprenticeship, often from a very young age, gradually developing manual dexterity and an intuitive sense of tools, materials, structure, proportion and aesthetics, until they became a holistic building expert.

In contrast, the practice of modern architecture is a three-fold process: analysing, imagining, and making. An architect analyses by collecting, documenting and mapping information, and then reflecting on and synthesising it. Following this, the results are translated into imagined forms and spaces using sketching, drawing, and model-making. Juhani Pallasmaa described the process as follows:

"While drawing, a mature designer and architect is not focused on the lines of the drawing, as he is envisioning the object itself, and in his mind holding the object in his hand and occupying the space being designed. During the design process, the architect occupies the very structure that the lines of the drawing represent … The architect moves about freely in the imagined structure, however large and complex it may be, as if walking in a building and touching all its surfaces and sensing their materiality and texture."[1]

In 2014, we were invited to exhibit some of our bamboo projects at Palazzo Bembo in Venice, as part of a concurrent programme of the 14th Architecture Biennale. We displayed miniature bamboo models and life-sized mock-ups supported by detailed drawings and images, all of which told a story about making. Built with satay sticks, the models were used to examine specific aspects of our architectural projects, such as structural composition and tectonics and how they affect the overall concept of a building, while also helping us to externalise ideas and put them into practice on a diminutive scale.

Opposite
Tukang building a malay kampung house

1

2

1 A *tukang* works mainly with natural materials

2 *Tanggam* connections are used to put together the timber structure in Malay kampung house

Not far from our little exhibit, at the Arsenale, was the Indonesian national exhibition, *Ketukangan: Kesadaran Material*, meaning "Craftsmanship: Material Consciousness". Against the persistent sound of building tools in use, the making of structures was explored through six common materials: timber, bamboo, brick, stone, concrete, and steel. Using text, moving images, and sound, the exhibition revealed how the craftsmanship and labour involved in handling each material has become an influence in developing the nation's architecture. I found these to have strong affinities with our bamboo display, where making was exposed as an instinctive way of working with materials that are cultivated, produced, selected and applied by local people in their own environment, using tools and techniques they have developed.

The process of thinking and exploring ideas through making is not explicitly expressed by our practice, but it remains an essential aspect of our daily architectural activity. In 2021, during the Covid pandemic, the lull of this period allowed us to think more deeply about how we do this. With a grant called "Connections through Culture", provided by the British Council, we embarked on a project that explores making and the craft of building in relation to material culture, building processes and engagement with local communities.[2]

The project began by recording conversations with three Malaysian *tukang*s, who are still practising the traditional method of building timber houses, to develop an understanding of their role, process and worldview. From this point of departure, we explored making in the work of contemporary architects and designers in the broader region of South East Asia, and in Britain. We spoke to Patcharada Inplang and Varudh Varavarn in Thailand, and Andy Rahman, Florian Heinzelmann and Daliana Suryawinata in Indonesia, while in the UK we consulted Rodrigo Garcia Gonzalez, Amin Taha and members of the 121 Collective.[3] There is an underlying commonality in the work of these practitioners, where each seeks to reference their distinctive culture, tradition, building method and climate through sustainable practices.

A few common threads emerged from these conversations: a conscious effort to explore and experiment with local and sustainable materials and building techniques, and to collaborate with local craftspeople to reach a deeper understanding of how to use them. These attitudes, and the work they produce, illustrates that working with what is at hand does not necessarily mean going back to pre-industrial ways of making, but, rather, opens up new possibilities for a post-industrial age while keeping local material culture and vernacular traditions dynamic.

This close connection with making was the default in architecture until the modern era's transition to specialisation and separation of design from the building process. Today, architects work in isolation away from the construction site, in their studio, with employees producing drawings and specifications instead of being directly immersed in the materials and process of making. Moreover, architectural education, with its growing emphasis on intellectualism and theoretical thinking, has created an additional distance between the studio and construction site, further diluting the principles of craft in the architect's work.

The process of architectural design has also changed considerably with technology. It is now possible to design a complete building in a matter of weeks using computer modelling software, without having to consider how building components are made, who made them or where they originated. Built into this software are standard building element catalogues, which enable three-dimensional walls, doors, windows, roofs, gutters, etc, to be added quickly to a building. Visualisations are accessible at the click of a button, with extraordinarily little room left to the imagination. When turning designs into physical buildings, this way of working has a trickle-down effect, encouraging the quick assembly of generic components, often high in embodied energy and made from materials extracted or produced in far-off places, to simplify the construction process.

As a practice, we love working with materials in their "as-found" state, which usually means as they are delivered, or in their early condition when first applied and before extra layers or coatings are added: unclad steel structures, bare concrete, clay bricks, wood and bamboo. Rather than imposing a preconceived idea or unnatural appearance on materials, we prefer to work to their unwritten rules, allowing each substance to fully express its individuality and physicality. Few of these materials are available in off-the-shelf prefabricated forms, and working with them is therefore based on the craftsperson's knowledge and dexterity, stemming from their usage in vernacular architecture. The contemporary architectural and construction industries believe this way of working belongs to the past, as it adds time and complexity. We, on the other hand, find it enriching, and prefer to celebrate a relationship with the construction team that is collaborative rather than authoritative and that avoids directing or controlling their activities.

We have attempted to adapt and develop this approach through our small pavilions. Almost all our pavilion projects are self-initiated, and are either built or managed by working collaboratively with small teams of craftspeople, builders, students and volunteers, in a way that gives us greater control over design and innovation and allows us to explore the potential of traditional methods and materials in contemporary forms.

The traditional *tanggam* method used in Malay houses was adopted in our Shadow Garden Pavilion, completed in 2016. The idea of growth, flexibility and impermanence is intrinsic to the timber architecture of this

1 Students developing Shadow Garden Pavilion's timber joints based on the *tanggam* method
2 Students assembling the Shadow Garden Pavilion
3 Shadow Garden Pavilion

1 3 4

2

1 Meranti Pavilion modules being fabricated by local craftspeople in a workshop in Malaysia
2 Meranti Pavilion was shipped and assembled in Orlando Florida
3 WUF09 Pavilion
4 WUF09 volunteers worked under the supervision of craftspeople

region, where sections cut from local Merbau or other wood are interlocked without the use of nails, screws or fasteners, to form a stable framed structure. A group of architecture students volunteered to help with the building work, and together we developed a series of mortise and tenon, dovetail, and keyed joints to create a timber structure based on the *tanggam* method, so it could be quickly assembled and dismantled on-site. A similar concept was used for the Meranti Pavilion (2017). Here, the pavilion needed to be designed in a way that would enable it to be moved from a workshop in Malaysia, where it was fabricated, to an exhibition hall in Orlando, Florida, for about three weeks, after which it would be dismantled and stored until required again. By working in close collaboration with skilled local carpenters, a series of standardised, modular components made from local Meranti wood was designed and fabricated. At the same time, several mock-ups were produced to determine the shape, size and weight of a module that could be easily handled and packed tightly into a shipping crate. The use of a simple interlocking joint system permitted the modules to be assembled quickly to form a 4 x 4 metre rectangular enclosure in less than 24 hours, using basic tools such as power drills and screwdrivers, and, if necessary, to be reassembled in different configurations, much like Lego bricks.

Similar to timber, bamboo is one of the oldest building resources but was never developed into a modern construction material. Our interest in bamboo led us to experiment with rings for the World Urban Forum 09 (WUF09) Pavilion, built in 2018 for an urban forum event organised by UN-Habitat in Kuala Lumpur. The different-sized and -shaped rings were cut from whole culms, cast off from another project, and packed tightly between vertical and horizontal bamboo frames to form wall claddings.

Coloured panels were then meticulously inserted into the small circular openings, resulting in embellished screens rich with texture. Here, a very old building material, rarely used in modern construction, was therefore reimagined as part of a new making system.

Similar interesting formations are seen in our IKN Pavilion, built in 2019, which was designed and constructed with craft students studying textile, metal, and wood crafts at a local craft institute. The students were asked to "adorn" a series of upright bamboo frames using their skills in innovative ways. Provided with bamboo, rattan, and hemp rope, in addition to a host of leftover craft materials teeming with hues and textures they found around their studios, they experimented with different techniques, such as weaving, plaiting and lashing. This collaborative and creative exchange generated interesting making methods that could be adapted to more complex applications.

1 Craft student working on IKN Bamboo Pavilion

2 Students were provided with natural materials such as bamboo, rattan and hemp ropes, in addition to a host of leftover craft materials

1

2

Our active involvement in building activities means that design development does not end before construction begins, but continues alongside it and trickles into the making process. For example, in the Bamboo Playhouse project (2015), we worked with skilled craftspeople versed in traditional bamboo jointing methods, using natural rope lashings to joint culms. Typically, rope lashings will decay and loosen over time, so a more durable solution was required. Working closely with the workers on-site as building work progressed, we created more efficient and durable jointing methods where lashings were combined with bolting and clamping, and also made prototypes and full-scale mock-ups to convey exactly what was required. This exchange has resulted in increased knowledge and safer, more resilient structures based on local materials.

The strategies described above can be considered part of a laissez-faire attitude that prevents a predetermined final state, and allows motivation and innovation to continue in tandem with the building process. Such an open-ended approach is easier to adopt in small-scale, self-built or self-managed projects, unlike more formal and highly controlled procedures such as a

1 2 | 3 4

1 The Bamboo Playhouse

2 Bamboo Playhouse column base detail

3 Bamboo Playhouse construction

4 Top of column detail in the Bamboo Playhouse

production line, where tasks are compartmentalised and conform to specific programmes. Though efficient, this more formal system depends on machine-fabricated and standardised building components.

In contrast to this, the cultural continuity and environmental awareness embodied in a form of making that is rooted in local methods can offer valuable insights into reimagining modern building practices. The making process involved in our timber and bamboo pavilions shapes form and construction beyond the aesthetic dimension, and allows us to tap into the skills and knowledge of traditional makers. Working in such a manner enriches architecture and catalyses a more profound social and cultural engagement between architect, maker, building user and the public realm.

ENDNOTES

1 Pallasmaa, Juhani, *The Thinking Hand: Existential and Embodied Wisdom in Architecture*, Hoboken, NJ: John Wiley & Sons Ltd, 2009, p 59.

2 "About Making" is a collaborative project that explores different aspects of "making" in art and architecture while carrying forward the materials and processes of traditional and modern craft in a cross-cultural and cross-disciplinary context. This project was undertaken by Dr Eleena Jamil and Kingston University academics Dr Christoph Lueder, Abbe Fletcher and Dr Stephen Knott, supported by the British Council: https://about-making.com/

3 Patcharada Inplang, together with partner Thongchai Chansamak, runs an architectural and building studio called Shermaker, in Chiangmai; Varudh Varavarn heads Vin Varavarn Architects Ltd, an architectural practice based in Bangkok, Thailand; Andy Rahman is an Indonesian architect based in Surabaya, Indonesia, and works with local materials, especially clay bricks. Both Florian Heinzelmann and Daliana Suryawinata are directors of SHAU, an architectural studio with offices in Indonesia, the Netherlands and Germany. Rodrigo Garcia Gonzalez is co-founder and co-CEO of Notpla, a London-based start-up that makes products such as edible packaging made of seaweed; Amin Taha is a London-based architect who founded the firm Groupwork, an employee ownership trust of which Taha is now chair; 121 Collective is a design-and-build collective based in southwest London and founded by Kingston University architecture graduates Salah Krichen and Pablo Feito Boirac, which specialises in small-scale architectural design projects.

Shadow Garden Pavilion

LOCATION
Shalini Ganendra Fine Art Gallery Residence, Petaling Jaya, Selangor

LATITUDE
3.1°N

YEAR
2016

THE PROJECT BEGAN with an invitation from Shalini Ganendra Fine Art Gallery to design and build a small pavilion in collaboration with a group of second-year architecture students from Taylor's University, Malaysia. Early conversations with Shalini, the gallery owner, centred around using a local hardwood timber called Merbau, and local building techniques. Ideas of what it means to build in this part of the world would also be explored with the students.

The art gallery is a residence-like two-storey structure with a U-shaped plan designed by Malaysian architect Ken Yeang, and acted as a test bed for his ecological design principles applied to a small building. The gallery spaces are arranged around a small central courtyard garden, which "is shaded from the sun in the afternoon and provides a comfortable micro-climate zone within the site",[1] and is also the location of the pavilion. The pavilion itself is a trellis-like timber structure measuring 3.4 metres high x 2.6 metres wide x 2.4 metres deep, a proportion that allows it to sit comfortably within the courtyard flanked by a pair of mature frangipani trees with pink flowers.

The Merbau structure was assembled using a traditional jointing method called *tanggam*, originally seen in traditional Malay timber houses. This method can best be described as an interlocking system that connects timber sections without using nails, screws or fasteners. Drawings illustrate the joints in great detail so that students, after going through a two-day course at the university

1 Working model of the pavilion
2 Interesting shadow patterns are cast on the ground by the pavilion and frangipani trees

1

2

The Shadow Garden Pavilion sits in the courtyard of the gallery

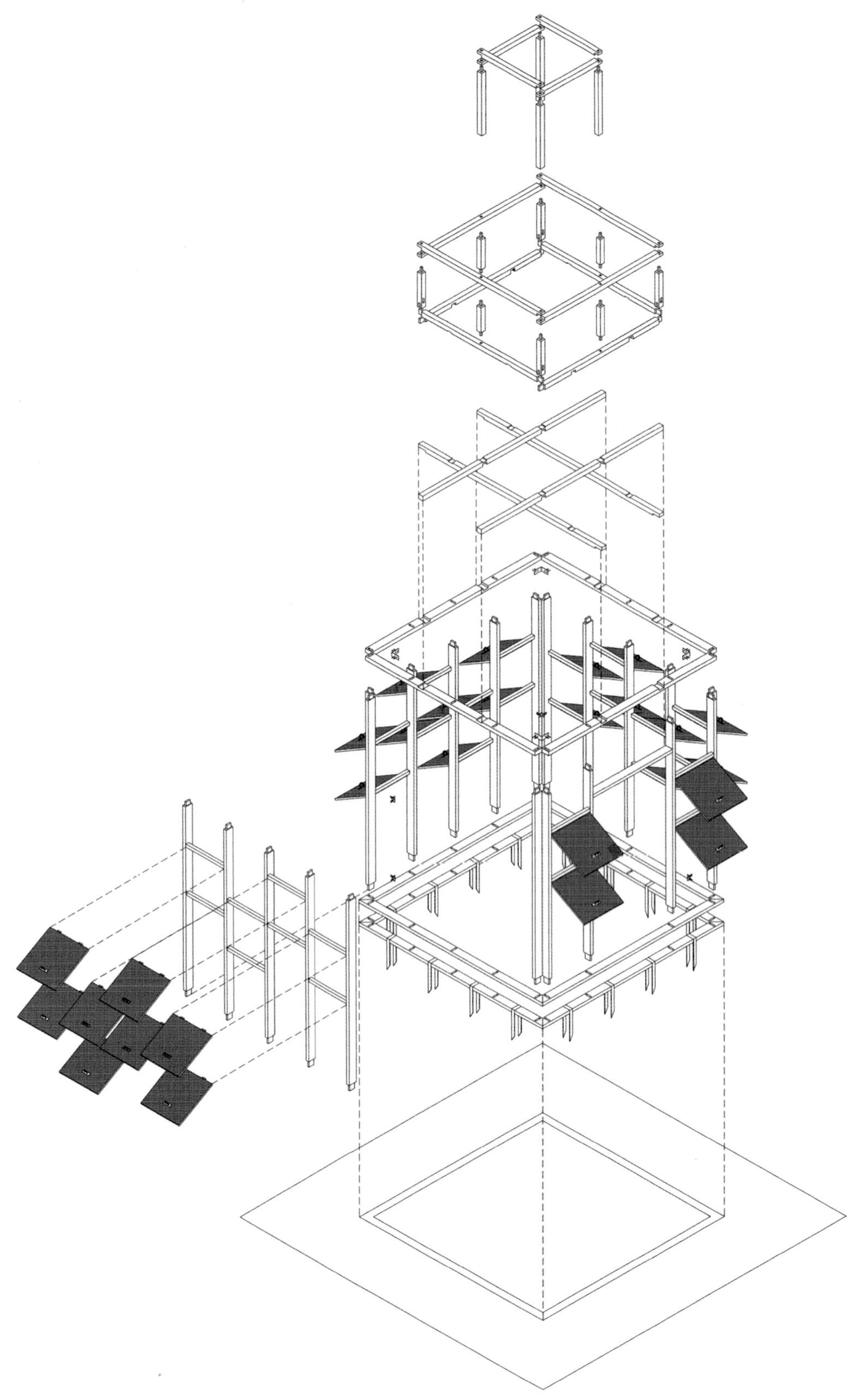

1 Detail drawing showing *tanggam* connections in the Shadow Garden Pavilion

2 Shutters are connected to planters using a simple pulley system

wood workshop, could cut timber sections to create an array of mortise and tenon, dovetail, and keyed joints based on the *tanggam* technique. Fabrication and assembly of the entire wooden structure took about three weeks to complete.

All four sides of the timber frame are hung with shutters made from galvanised steel plates. Each shutter is connected to a hanging box planter using a rope-and-pulley system, which allows the opening and closing of shutters to move the planters up and down. When combined with the frangipanis, these create an interesting shadow pattern around the pavilion. The planters are filled with aromatic local herbs and plants typically used for cooking or associated with healing properties.

In a whimsical way, the Shadow Garden Pavilion speaks of a building in a particular place. Merbau wood is locally available, and the *tanggam* technique refers to the regional tradition of making. The moving shutters relate to the need for shade and cool in a hot tropical climate, while the plants provide a sensory and visual experience unique to this part of the world.

ENDNOTE

1 As described by Dr Ken Yeang and his team, https://trhamzahyeang.com/portfolio-item/ganendra-art-house/, accessed December 2023.

World Urban Forum 09 (WUF09) Pavilion

FIRST LOCATION
Near Medan Pasar,
Kuala Lumpur

CURRENT LOCATION
Courtyard of Kulliyyah
of Architecture and
Environmental Design,
International Islamic
University Malaysia

YEAR
2018

LATITUDE
3.1°N

THE MEETING POINT of the Klang and Gombak Rivers is said to be the location of where Kuala Lumpur, which bears the meaning "muddy confluence", was founded. The area is surrounded and defined by colonial masonry buildings with decorative mouldings, and modern edifices inspired by the International Style. At the juncture of the two rivers is Jamek Mosque, built in 1909 and designed by Arthur Benison Hubback, a British architect and soldier, in the neo-Mughal style adopted by the British in India and other colonial regions. The WUF09 Pavilion was placed at the confluence of the rivers and directly south of the mosque for a week-long UN Habitat-organised 9th World Urban Forum hosted by the city, before it was moved to its permanent home at International Islamic University's architecture faculty.

Commissioned by UN-Habitat, the small structure makes a bold statement about local materiality and culture. It is made almost entirely from bamboo, one of the oldest building materials in the region, in its most natural

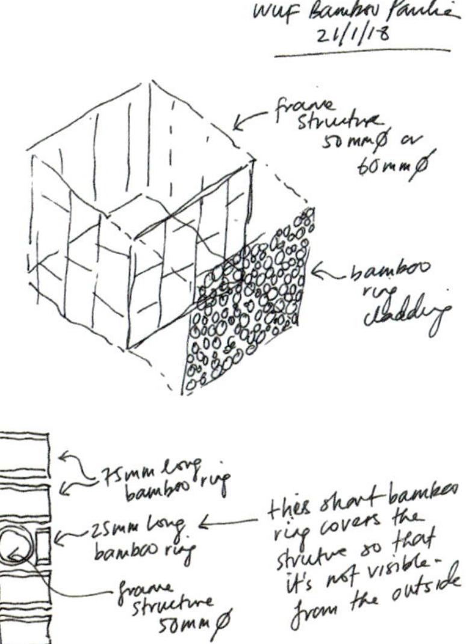

1 The pavilion's walls are made of bamboo rings with colourful inserts
2 Sketch of bamboo rings' installation
3 Column detail

1 The pavilion's first location was in a public space surrounded by modern and colonial buildings

2 Detail of the post and beam connection

3 Close-up of the bamboo rings lit up at night

state, that is, whole culms, and therefore offers a more sustainable alternative to the masonry, steel and glass of the buildings surrounding it. The form is contemporary: a simple cube with four framed walls filled with bamboo rings cut from culms left over from a previous project. Some of the rings are inserted with coloured panels, creating a decorative effect that alludes to the hues used to categorise UN Sustainable Development Goals.

The budget for the pavilion was meagre, but it presented a rare opportunity to be fully involved in design and production and led to working closely with local bamboo crafts-builders, young architects and ecologically conscious youths, who all rolled up their sleeves to help build the structure. There were a lot of discussions on-site about how to put the rings together and how to insert the coloured panels, which proved to be time-consuming considering that no two rings are alike. However, the intention was to replicate a modern design with local knowledge and materials.

IKN Pavilion

LOCATION
National Craft Institute,
Rawang, Selangor,
Malaysia

YEAR
2019

LATITUDE
3.2°N

MALAYSIAN ARCHITECTURAL CRAFT is based on natural and locally found materials. For example, the decorative carved panels seen in traditional houses are made from hardwood trees; intricate jewellery is fashioned from silver; woven baskets and mats from rattan, bamboo and screw pine leaves; whereas cooking pots and pumpkin-shaped water vessels are moulded from clay.

The idea of exploring natural materials was the premise of a week-long pop-up studio held with craft students at the local National Craft Institute. Under our guidance, students from the weaving, ceramic, woodwork, metalwork and batik studios were tasked with finding innovative ways to complete four sets of framed bamboo structures, using natural materials such as bamboo rings, split rattan, and hemp strings, and objects found around their studio such as yarn, fabric, metal wires and pieces of wood. The students were asked to draw inspiration from their studio work and the local surroundings, as well as from traditional and contemporary motifs, forms and techniques.

Their work resulted in a wondrously colourful and vibrant pavilion, bursting with ideas and techniques. Materials such as bamboo, rattan, wood, metal and strings were interlaced, like fabric, to become tactile surfaces that offered shade and privacy, framed views, and created the possibility of a community-based architecture rooted in local craft.

For many of the students, it was the first time they had worked with bamboo and rattan. For us, working with craft students has expanded our viewpoint and provided inspiration for our own work. Here, the act of thinking by making seen in craft became part of the architectural process, while innovation occurred through complementary activities such as sketching and drawing.

1 Students were provided with simple bamboo frame structures to complete using natural materials and objects found around their studio

2 Introducing students to bamboo, as many are not familiar with it as building or craft material

1

2

1

2

1–2 The pavilion was completed with interesting textures and colours

Meranti Pavilion

LOCATION
Expo, AIA Conference on Architecture 2017, Orlando, Florida

YEAR
2017

LATITUDE
28.5°N

1 Timber modules packed for shipping

2 Custom butterfly-shaped connectors are used to hold the corners together

MERANTI IS ONE of South East Asia's strongest hardwood species capable of structural use, and the pavilion is designed to demonstrate its strength, beauty and versatility as a sustainable building material. Commissioned by the Malaysian Timber Council, the design brief called for a flexible structure that could be easily assembled in locations around the world, and dismantled for storage when not in use. The first location was at the expo that ran concurrently with the AIA Conference on Architecture 2017 in Orlando, Florida.

The design of the pavilion is based on the concept of modularity, with each module approximately 700mm high x 600mm wide x 165mm deep, making it small enough to be handled by one person and easy to assemble and transport to other locations, and crafted by skilled Malaysian carpenters after exploring different mock-ups with us. There are 232 identical modules in total, which are stacked, slotted and then screwed together to form a simple rectangular pavilion of 3.4 metres high x 6 metres wide x 6 metres deep. Dismantling involves the same process in reverse. There are no vertical columns or beams to hold up the pavilion; instead, the modular elements work together in an interlocking system to give stability to the overall structure. The corners are held together by a unique butterfly-shaped metal component, which links the pavilion walls at the corners of each module.

The Meranti Pavilion is lattice-like, with a repeating motif of overlapping squares and protruding rectangular sections in a three-dimensional arrangement. This geometrical pattern of Meranti wood in its natural colour of rich reddish brown refers to the intricacy of traditional local woodwork.

The Meranti Pavilion assembled at a local workshop before it was dismantled and shipped to Orlando

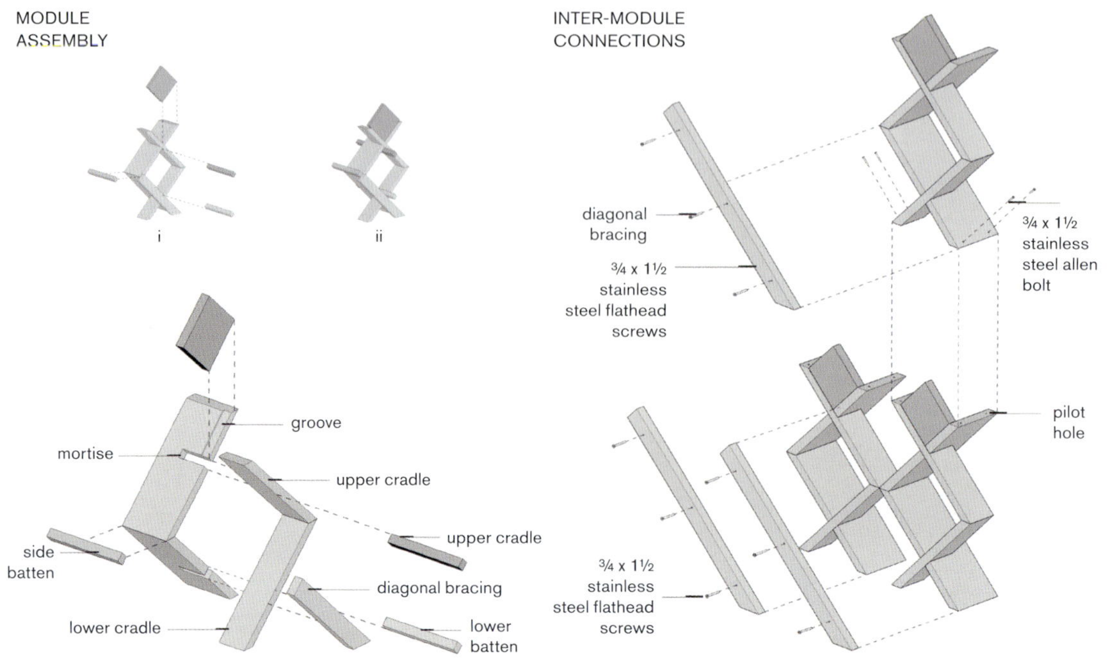
MODULE
ASSEMBLY
i
ii
groove
mortise
upper cradle
upper cradle
side
batten
diagonal bracing
lower cradle
lower
batten
INTER-MODULE
CONNECTIONS
diagonal
bracing
3/4 x 1 1/2
stainless
steel flathead
screws
3/4 x 1 1/2
stainless
steel allen
bolt
pilot
hole
3/4 x 1 1/2
stainless
steel flathead
screws

1

2 3

1 The pavilion is lattice-like, with a repeating motif of overlapping timber sections
2 Modular components of Meranti Pavilion
3 The pavilion as assembled in the workshop where it was fabricated

Bamboo as a Building Material

Our search for ways to build sustainably and contextually within South East Asia has led us to use bamboo as a building material. Bamboo is an accessible source, as the plant thrives locally and grows remarkably quickly at less than a quarter the rate of growing trees for lumber. It is also one of the few natural building materials that can be harvested and used almost immediately with minimal processing, all of which make its carbon footprint extremely low. Light in weight, it is easy to manage on-site with simple tools and without the use of heavy machinery.

Bamboo has always been part of the everyday life of communities living close to where the plant grows. The significance of the plant to the native people of the Hill Tracts of Chittagong in Bangladesh is described by Thomas H Lewin, a British colonial administrator, in his book of 1869:

"The bamboo is literally his staff of life. He builds his house of the bamboo; he fertilizes his fields with its ashes; of its stem he makes vessels in which to carry water; with two bits of bamboo, he can produce fire; its young and succulent shoots provide a dainty dinner dish; and he weaves his sleeping mat of fine slips thereof. The instruments with which his women weave their cotton are of bamboo. He makes drinking cups of it, and his head at night rests on a bamboo pillow; his forts are built of it; he catches fish, makes baskets, and stools, and thatches his house with the help of the bamboo. He smokes from a pipe of bamboo and from bamboo ashes he obtains potash. Finally, his funeral pile is lighted with bamboo."[1]

Vernacular bamboo structures derive from a complete understanding of the potential of the material and of how people live and work, and provide insight into how we could build more sustainably according to the opportunities and constraints of a local material. Examples of these structures can be found in many communities. For instance, bamboo stilt houses are built by the *Mru* indigenous people, who live in the Chittagong Hill Tracts, the hilly border region in south-eastern Bangladesh.[2] In the Philippines, the material is used to build *gunu bong* – large single-volume *T'boli* dwellings housing more than 20 people, raised on stilts by about 2 metres above ground.[3] In Ethiopia, the indigenous

1 | 2

1 Mru Village in the Chittagong Hill Tracts of Bangladesh
2 Mru House interior

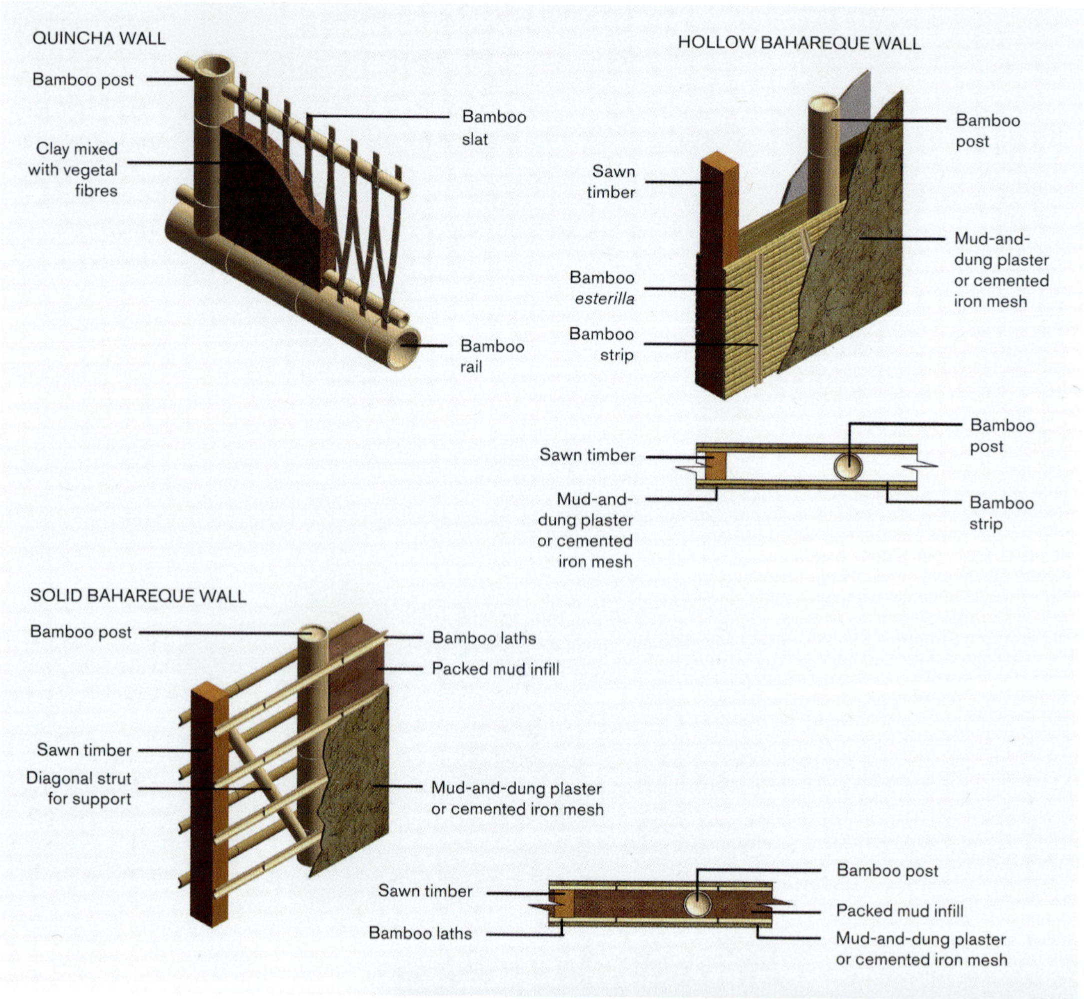

QUINCHA WALL

Bamboo post
Bamboo slat
Clay mixed with vegetal fibres
Bamboo rail

HOLLOW BAHAREQUE WALL

Bamboo post
Sawn timber
Mud-and-dung plaster or cemented iron mesh
Bamboo *esterilla*
Bamboo strip

Sawn timber
Bamboo post
Mud-and-dung plaster or cemented iron mesh
Bamboo strip

SOLID BAHAREQUE WALL

Bamboo post
Bamboo laths
Packed mud infill
Sawn timber
Diagonal strut for support
Mud-and-dung plaster or cemented iron mesh

Sawn timber
Bamboo post
Packed mud infill
Bamboo laths
Mud-and-dung plaster or cemented iron mesh

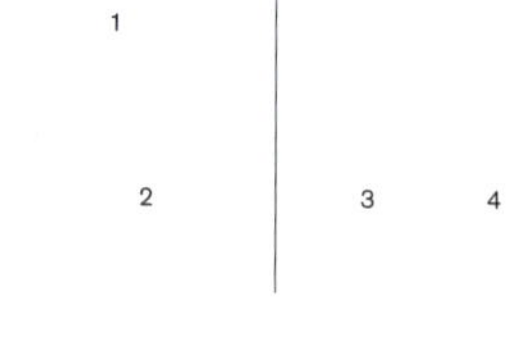

1 South American wattle-and-daub wall construction

2 Bamboo processing workshop run by a local indigenous community

3 Bamboo culm morphology

4 Bamboo curing methods involve soaking the fibres with treatment solution. There are different ways to achieve this: i. steeping method ii. open tank immersion method (used in the bamboo playhouse) iii. pressure impregnation method

Cechen (Dorze) and *Sidama* people construct dwellings that function as both home and barn, and are woven like bamboo baskets in the shapes of cones and domes.[4] In vernacular South American buildings, bamboo is used as part of wattle-and-daub wall construction, where it is interlaced and fixed in place with mixes of mud, earth, clay and animal excrement, and finished with plaster. This system is known as *quincha* in Peru,[5] and in Colombia as *bahareque.*[6] In Hong Kong, bamboo culms are used as scaffolding in the construction of buildings, a tradition that can be traced back to the Han Dynasty (202 BC–220 AD), where scenes of *peng ge* or bamboo scaffolds are depicted in brick and stone reliefs in ancient tombs.[7]

The use of bamboo rapidly disappeared from construction with the introduction of modern materials such as concrete and steel. One of the main reasons for this was because bamboo was regarded as a "poor man's" material, meaning no attempt was made to improve its practicability and durability beyond rudimentary use. It is now known that bamboo can have a long life if appropriately cured and is a well-engineered plant with a hollow morphological structure evolving from the need to resist wind and snow loads, and achieves stability and stiffness with the least amount of material. These attributes result from its longitudinal fibres that have high tensile strength, earning it the nickname "green steel". As an architectural practice, we are particularly fascinated by the way bamboo fails when bending. When a culm fails, it does not break clean like timber, where the first crack will lead to a total fracture into two pieces. Instead, the longitudinal fibres start to separate but return to their original tubular form once the load is removed, keeping the structure intact.[8]

On account of its ease and cost-effectiveness as a building material, bamboo has long been embraced by local communities as a viable, eco-friendly option. For our Bamboo Playhouse (2015), culms were sourced from a group of *orang asli* – local indigenous people running a small bamboo workshop located on the fringe of a forest in Raub, Pahang, about two hours' drive from our Kuala Lumpur project site. Turning them into a building material begins by removing branches and leaves, and then cleaning the outer walls by rubbing sand onto them mixed with water. This is followed by a "curing" process,

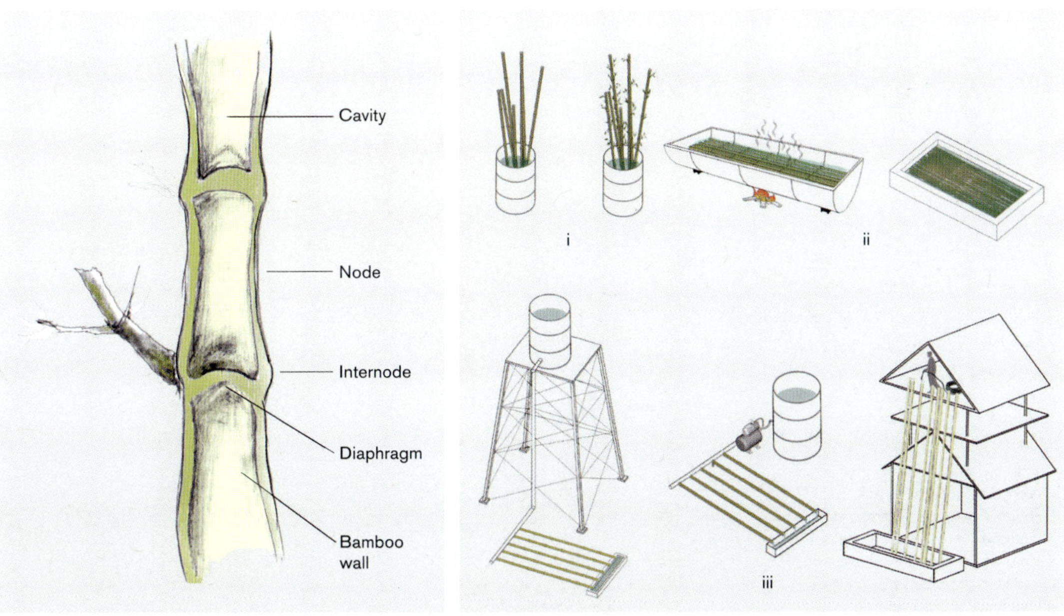

which involves immersing the culms in a tank filled with treatment solution for several days, to ensure the cellulosic fibres are thoroughly soaked and the starch content is removed to make them less attractive to insects. The next step is to dry them slowly and thoroughly in an upright position in a well-ventilated space under a roof for a couple of months.

The curing process described above is one of the simplest methods and is suitable for bamboo in its most natural state, that is, whole round culms, or split or cut sections, as seen in our work. The process varies from the most rudimentary methods, such as smoking culms, soaking them in the river and drying them out in the open, generally without using chemicals, to highly processed ones that involve impregnating culms with solutions using pressure through mechanisation or a vacuum.

Curing bamboo is not sufficient alone to ensure durability. Like most natural building materials, its life is extended considerably by keeping it dry. Culms in contact with water for prolonged periods will lead to decay, as moisture is constantly absorbed along their cellulosic vessels. This requires the material to avoid contact with the ground, which can get damp during rainy seasons, and to be placed under roof cover. In our Bamboo Classroom project, completed in 2010, all bamboo columns sit under a roof with large overhangs and are placed 500mm above ground on a raised concrete deck. Here, slim metal bars are cast into the deck, of which 550mm is left protruding at a pre-determined angle, ready to receive the culms. Once the culms are

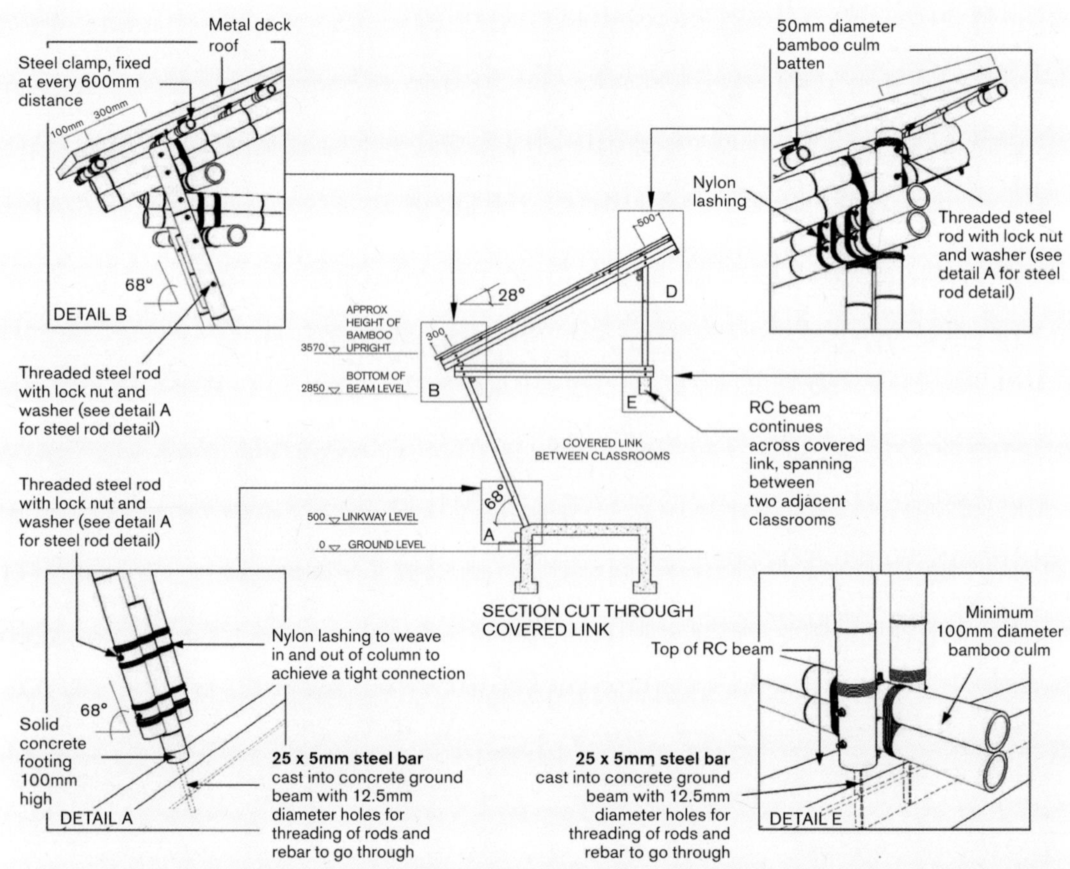

lowered onto the bars, bolts are then threaded horizontally through both the bamboo and bars, and mortar is injected into the cavity of the culms to ensure strong connections with the ground deck.

A similar approach can be seen in the Bamboo Playhouse. All the bamboo columns are placed on circular concrete stumps that rise from the middle of an elevated concrete deck to keep them dry. Each stump has a profile that slopes downwards along the edges, to throw off excess rainwater. As in the classroom, metal bars are cast into the concrete stump, with approximately 500mm protruding upwards, ready to receive the culms which are lowered onto the bars and then filled with mortar, and lashed.

As no two culms are alike, their jointing techniques differ vastly from other building materials. We usually use popular traditional methods of jointing, brilliantly described and illustrated by Colombian architect Oscar Hidalgo Lopez in his seminal *Manual de construcción con bambú*, published in 1981.[9] In this method, the rigidity of joints relies heavily on the friction between culms, which are cut and carved manually on-site to form a specific shape that allows them to be saddled onto the curved surface of another. Some common cuts include the "single-flange", "double-flange", bevelled, "fluted-mouth" and "fish-mouth", and ensure a very close fit when jointing two or more culms together. Typically, the joints are then completed by rope lashings, using natural materials such as thinned split bamboo, coco-fibre, cotton, coir, jute, or rattan, and synthetic fibres such as nylon or polyethylene. The lashings tend to deteriorate faster than bamboo or unravel after some time, so we overcome this by applying a resin layer to the lashings to keep them intact for longer.

In our bamboo structures, these traditional jointing methods are supplemented with additional techniques to further strengthen the connections. For our Bamboo Classroom building, for example, located in the Philippines' Bicol Peninsula where wind speeds can reach as high as 200km/h during tropical storms or typhoons, the structure demanded extra strengthening. Apart from mortar injected into the base of the bamboo columns, as described

1 Detail drawing of bamboo joints for the Bamboo Classroom
2 Column detail in the Bamboo Playhouse
3 Stumps with reinforcement bars ready to receive the culms in the Bamboo Playhouse
4 Bamboo Classroom column detail
5 Bamboo Classroom's jointing detail

above, we also used nuts and bolts. Connections between two or more culms are first made by shaping and notching the ends for a snug fit, to prevent them from slipping as the result of friction. Bolts with rubber washers, some combined with a hook to connect to another bamboo running perpendicular, are then threaded through the culms. These joints are designed to allow a small amount of movement, with the washers acting like dampers to absorb wind energy.

Another example where additional strengthening is required can be seen in the Bamboo Playhouse, where custom-designed connectors are used to reinforce the corners of bamboo baskets hung centrally from bamboo columns. These connectors take the form of three-pronged welded metal pipes, into which the ends of the culms are inserted. Placing these connectors on all four corners provided much-needed rigidity for the cantilever, but, covered by rope lashings, they remain invisible in the completed building.

NATURAL OR ENGINEERED BAMBOO?

Working with bamboo in its near-natural state, in the form of either whole culms, or split or cut sections, means having to deal with wide dimensional variations. Each culm is hollow, tapers significantly from base to tip, has nodes at varying distances, non-uniform cross sections, and a wide range of mechanical properties along its length. It is unlike working with engineered bamboo, which is highly processed and often involves segmenting, splitting and planing, followed by treating (steaming, carbonisation or bleaching, and subsequent drying), and, finally, by heat pressing or laminating to become planks, boards, structural beams and columns, to provide uniform strength and modularity. However, we favour culms in our work for their much lower energy footprint in transforming them from a plant to a viable building material.

Our methods of jointing bamboo culms, involving friction-tight lashings supplemented with bolting and grouting, remain a vernacular- and craft-based practice that is performed in-situ, with the quality and strength of connections dependent on the skill of the worker rather than on precise mechanical calculations. This system works remarkably well in small- and medium-sized projects, but is impractical in large developments, as it can add significantly to construction time and costs. A compromise is therefore required to allow bamboo in its near-natural state to be used for sustainable low-carbon developments. The answer lies in engineering the connections between culms.

Numerous studies have been conducted with the aim of increasing the efficiency of culm connections by developing joint hubs and connectors made from materials such as timber,[10] steel,[11,12] PVC (Polyvinyl Chloride) and FRP (Fibre Reinforced Polymer),[13] to maintain the lightweight nature of bamboo construction. In most of these cases, the ends of culms are inserted into or bolted with connectors so they can be joined in different directions. This approach avoids relying on direct culm-to-culm connections and has the potential to be modular, leading the way towards a more straightforward plug-and-build construction process. A different approach can be seen in the "Energy Efficient Bamboo House" project in China, by Studio Cardenas, where "dry connections" have been developed to prevent weakening the bamboo by bolting.[14] Here, bamboo culms are sandwiched between lightweight aluminium plates and held in position by bolts that thread through the plates.

These "engineered" jointing systems permit the efficient assembly of a structure where whole culms of varying sizes and shapes can be easily connected, and eliminate, almost entirely, the need to shape and profile the ends of culms to achieve a close fit at the joints. They thus considerably reduce the need for on-site manual labour, and will encourage more sustainable developments where minimally processed bamboo culms, harvested locally, can be used in large projects such as mass housing, and workplace and educational developments.

1

2

1 Bamboo Playhouse's custom designed connectors

2 Industrialised jointing system
a) Albermani, Goh & Chan
b) Obermann & Laude
c) Bambutec
d) Guaduatech
e) Studio Cardenas

MATERIAL OF THE FUTURE

Bamboo is considered one of the most ecologically sustainable building materials, particularly when used in its near-natural form and sourced within short distances. Using it in mass developments such as housing, schools and offices could contribute significantly to tackling climate change, yet it remains a material of the past and future. Its widespread use in modern construction is confronted with countless difficulties: restrictive regulations, lack of national standards, building codes, and a bureaucracy that encourages standardised solutions. These obstacles are further hampered by insufficient research into fire resistance and material grading, lack of co-ordination between stakeholders, and a dominant techno style that tends to curb alternative creativity in favour

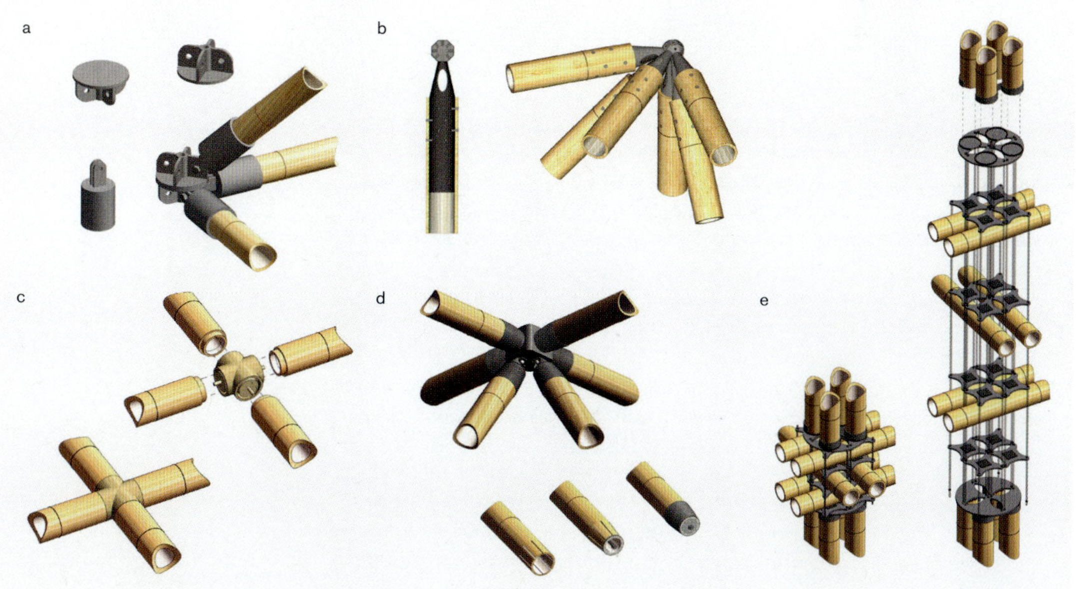

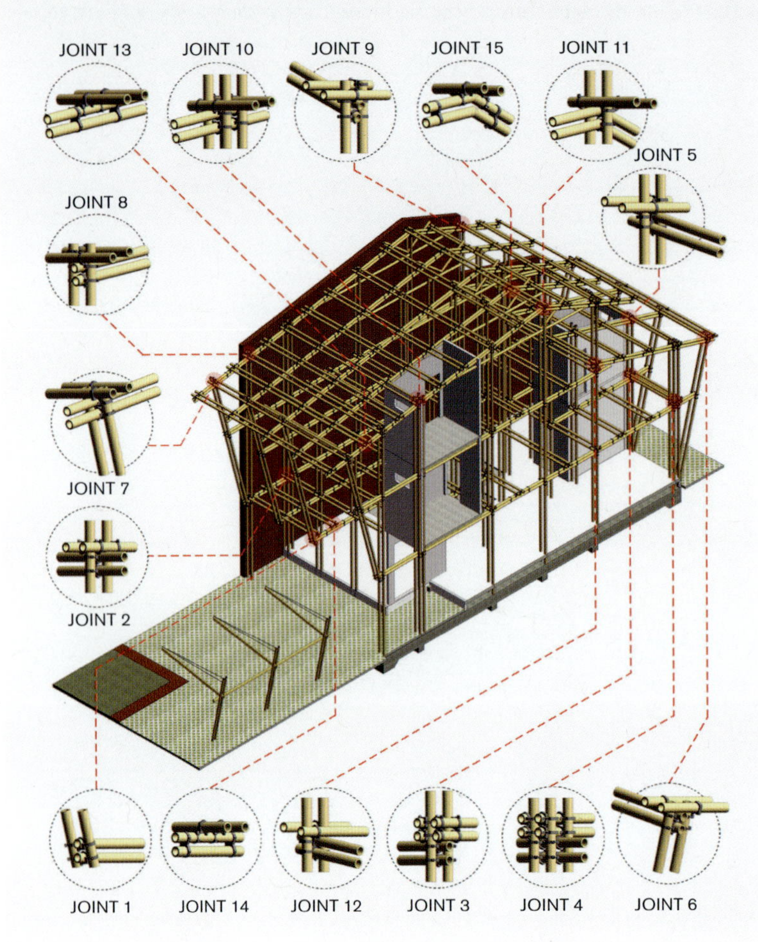

Left
Jointing system using steel clamps are being developed for the bamboo terrace homes

of the practices of multinational corporations. Trying to build successfully with bamboo means first having to combat these impediments.

The Bamboo Terrace Home is our proposal to raise awareness of the potential of bamboo in mass housing. Developed in-house in 2018 without a client, the project examines the use of structural bamboo in exchange for concrete in a contemporary typology: the Malaysian terrace house, in this case one that is 22ft wide and two-and-a-half storeys high. Except for the concrete slab floor, which is slightly raised to provide a dry base for the house to sit on, the entire structure of the building is made from bamboo culms jointed together with modular steel connectors, and that span the masonry walls between adjoining houses. These walls provide the breaks necessary to contain fire from spreading across the entire row. Performing very much like timber platform frames, culms of different sizes form columns and beams, onto which are set bamboo floor joists and wall studs. These are then clad with composite bamboo panels to create flat and seamless interior surfaces for receiving a range of contemporary finishes, such as plaster and paint, wallpaper, laminate and veneers.

Developing connection details that are straightforward, inexpensive and quick to assemble is vital to the viability of bamboo housing. We started by looking at existing technologies that could be easily adapted to the project and were struck by the efficacy of the tubular scaffolding system. Here, steel poles are quickly assembled by highly modularised clamps and couplers, which allow poles to be fixed in different directions.

This scaffolding system suggests that a method for jointing the culms could be developed without mortar injections and bolting, involving specially designed steel clamps, which would allow greater versatility and preservation of material integrity. A thin layer of heavy-duty, rubberised material lines the inner surface of the clamp to provide the friction necessary to keep the irregularly shaped and sized culms from slipping. Each clamp is connected to another of the same with a swivel joint to form a "coupler", while variations in the joint allow for connections in different directions. The system also enables damaged culms – split, cracked or decayed – to be replaced when required. In an era when industrialisation of architecture and construction is much criticised for causing climate change, here it can be used for the greater good. The clamps can be prefabricated in factories and assembled on-site in a relatively simple, Lego-like process.

A GREEN SHIFT

Climate change demands shifts in the way we build. Using bamboo as a building material, particularly in the form of whole culms, and in places where the plant thrives, offers a greener alternative to industrially produced materials that depend on high energy consumption. Bamboo and natural building materials such as straw, hemp, wool, cork, vegetable fibres and mycelium mushrooms are sustainable, have a low carbon footprint and generate zero waste so can be composted after use. We take particular comfort in the notion of circular thinking and in the potential of feeding building materials back into the biological cycle of the earth.

Bamboo plants thrive in regions where the greatest amount of urbanisation is taking place, so encouraging the material's use at a larger scale will significantly contribute to reducing global carbon emissions. As a practice based in South East Asia, it is just as important for us that the use of bamboo relates to the local and cultural context, reduces dependence on imported and non-renewable materials, and generates employment among workers.

ENDNOTES

1 Lewin, Thomas H, *The Hill Tracts of Chittagong and the Dwellers Therein: With Comparative Vocabularies of the Hill Dialects*, Calcutta: Bengal Print Co Ltd, 1869, pp 9–10.

2 Brauns, CD and LG Löffler, *Mru: Hill People on the Border of Bangladesh*, Basel: Brikhauser, 1990.

3 Talavera, MJP, "The T'boli: Songs, Stories and Society", *Anthropology 1*, Summer 2013; Corazon, H, "The Ethnic Tradition", *CCP Encyclopedia of Philippine Art*, NG Tiongson, ed, Manila: Cultural Centre of the Philippines, 1994; CCP Encyclopedia of Philippine Art: Philippine architecture - Cultural Center of the Philippines - Google Books.

4 Olmstead, J, "The Dorze House: A Bamboo Basket", *Journal of Ethiopian Studies*, vol 10, no 2, 1972; "Dorze Huts of Woven Bamboo", The Art Section uk/Nomad Architecture, http://artsection.org/dorze.html, accessed 13 July 2021; Darge, A and DA Nuramo, "Ethiopian Vernacular Bamboo Architecture and its Potentials for Adaptation in Modern Urban Housing: A Case Study", *Fifth International Conference on Sustainable Construction Materials and Technologies*, London, July 2019; Midekessa, I, "Sidama House Construction", https://www.youtube.com/watch?v=Y-CrVa3ZKjU, accessed July 2021.

5 Carbajal, F, G Ruiz, and CJ Schexnayder, "Quincha Construction in Peru", *Practice Periodical on Structural Design and Construction*, vol 10, no 1, February 2005; Witte, D, "Contemporary Bamboo Housing in South America: Challenges and Opportunities for Building in the Informal Sector" (thesis), University of Washington, 2018.

6 Parsons, JJ, "Giant American Bamboo in the Vernacular Architecture of Colombia and Ecuador", *The Geographical Review*, vol 81, no 2, April 1991, pp 131–52.

7 Lau, SHF, *Rethinking Bamboo – Aspects of Contemporary Design*, Hong Kong: Asia One Books, 2013.

8 Janssen, JA, *Designing and Building with Bamboo, Technical Report 20*, Beijing: International Network for Bamboo and Rattan, 2000, pp 20–24.

9 Lopez, OH, *Manual de construcción con bambú (Manual of Bamboo Construction)*, Universidad Nacional de Colombia, Estudios Técnicos Colombianos, Ltda, 1981.

10 For example, Germany-based Bambutec uses cnc-milled timber hubs that could be used to joint tubular bamboo culms and timber, "Bambutec", https://bambutec.eu/technology.

11 For example, Obermann developed a steel tube with a conical end, which is inserted into the culm and bolted into the steel connecting hub. The steel tube prevents collapse of the culm wall, and the bolts transfer the forces to the bamboo fibres. Obermann, TM, and R Laude, "Bamboo Poles for Spatial and Light Structures", Bamboo-Space Research Project, Universidad Nacional de Colombia, Sede Medellin – Technische Universität Berlin, Germany, 2004.

12 Developed and patented by Guaduatech, the ends of culms are engineered to allow for easy jointing to other culms or mediums, such as steel and concrete. Here, steel wires are wound tight around the end of pinched culms, allowing a protruding screw to connect to different hub configurations. Lodoño, J, "Method for preparing a terminal assembly for bamboo", Washington, DC: US Patent 6,957,479 B2, 25 October 2005.

13 Albermani F, G Goh and S-L Chan, "Lightweight Bamboo Double Layer Grid System", *Engineering Structures*, vol 29, 2007, pp 1499–1506.

14 "Studio Cardenas: Energy Efficient Bamboo House", https://www.studiocardenas.it/index.php/en/2015-03-23-13-40-30/housing/148-energy-efficient-bamboo-house, accessed October 2022.

The Bamboo Playhouse

LOCATION
Perdana Botanical Gardens,
Kuala Lumpur, Malaysia

YEAR
2015

LATITUDE
3.1°N

NESTLED BETWEEN THE clusters of tall glass towers that have come to define Asian cities is a patch of hilly garden known as Lake Garden, established during the colonial era in 1887.[1] Its original name refers to the large green lake at its centre, visible for miles around, but it is now known as Perdana Botanical Gardens. Much loved by locals and frequented by tourists, the park is one of the most important green lungs in a city that grows continually in density and height.

In early 2014, Kuala Lumpur City Hall approached us to design a visitor pavilion for the Botanical Gardens, to serve as a rest and activity space for visitors. We saw this as an opportunity to explore bamboo as a primary building material, and set out to design an open "playful" structure referencing the traditional pavilion typology known as *wakaf*. In its most basic form, a *wakaf* is a simple four-posted structure, open on all sides, with a pitched roof and a raised floor a few steps up from the ground. It is made from natural materials such as timber, bamboo and thatch and can be found where people live and along travel routes, encouraging passers-by to stop and rest under its shade.

1 The Bamboo Playhouse is a pavilion inspired by the traditional pavilion typology known as "wakaf"

2 Bird's-eye view of the pavilion, with photovoltaic panels on the roof

The Playhouse sits on one of the small islands in the park's lake and consists of 31 little *wakafs*, each with a cantilevered concrete floor deck of 3.2 square metres, set at different levels along diagonal gridlines close to the water's edge. From the centre of each platform rises a bunch of tightly wound bamboo columns, at the top of which bamboo rafters support a sizeable single-plane, metal-deck roof mounted with photovoltaic panels. Below these, the ceiling soffits are lined with woven bamboo mats. Four bamboo baskets, akin to treehouses, are attached halfway up the columns of the main structure, accessed by bamboo ladders.

The visitor route in the botanical gardens passes through the Bamboo Playhouse, leading visitors to its island across white masonry bridges. On this island are clusters of palms and bamboo plants of varied species, creating an interesting backdrop to the structure. With its unique form and materiality, the Playhouse has proved popular with visitors, who often stop to rest on the multiple platforms or in the treehouses shaded from the tropical sun, to cool down before moving on to explore the park. Countless activities have been organised here, from children's birthday parties to corporate events.

ENDNOTE

1 In 1511, Malacca fell into the hands of the Portuguese, an event that marked the beginning of the colonial era in Malaya. In 1641, Malaya fell to the Dutch, and in 1824 to the British via the Anglo–Dutch Treaty. British colonisation was the longest, lasting for more than 100 years until the country gained independence in August 1957, when it became known as Malaysia.

1 Activities are often held at the Bamboo Playhouse such as children's parties and corporate events

2 Typical detail of raised decks

3 The pavilion sits close to the water's edge

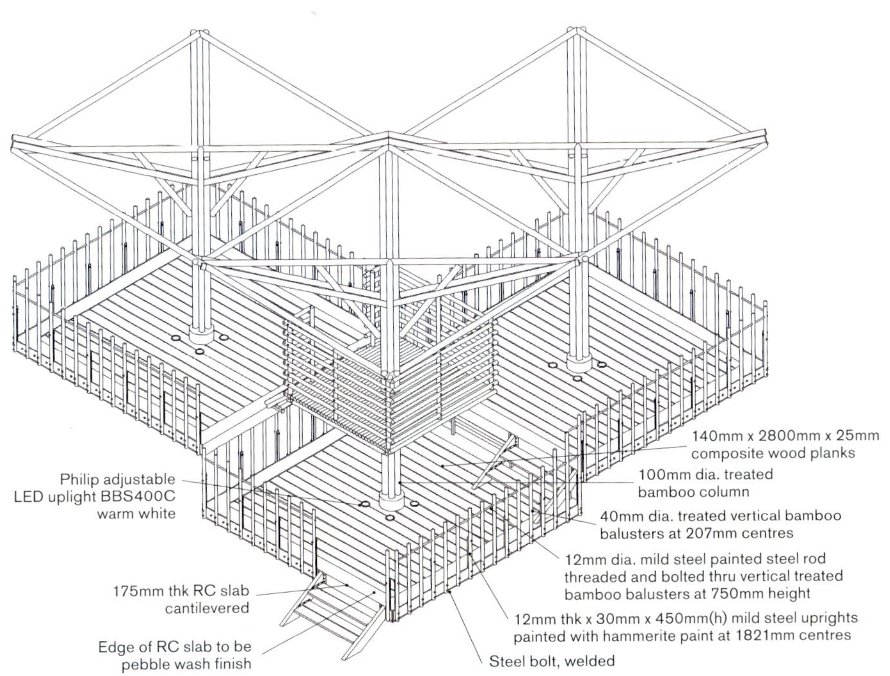
140mm x 2800mm x 25mm
composite wood planks
100mm dia. treated
bamboo column
Philip adjustable
LED uplight BBS400C
warm white
40mm dia. treated vertical bamboo
balusters at 207mm centres
12mm dia. mild steel painted steel rod
threaded and bolted thru vertical treated
bamboo balusters at 750mm height
175mm thk RC slab
cantilevered
12mm thk x 30mm x 450mm(h) mild steel uprights
painted with hammerite paint at 1821mm centres
Edge of RC slab to be
pebble wash finish
Steel bolt, welded

Building a Playhouse

WE SELDOM USE bamboo for every element in a building. When we do, it is to create hybrid structures, where parts are designed more innovatively using bamboo, in combination with other standard materials such as steel, concrete or bricks. This is a way to reduce risks to our clients, who often worry about durability and maintenance. Hybrid structures tend to have a much longer service life, as threats such as insect and fungal attack, and moisture-related degradation, are easier to deal with. For the Bamboo Playhouse, placing all culms on and above raised concrete decks eliminated contact with ground moisture, while a metal deck roof provided a more protective and long-lasting cover than a roof made from bamboo or other natural material. In terms of connections, we often combine culms with metal and concrete to provide strength and rigidity.

When the Bamboo Playhouse was built in 2014, there were very few bamboo buildings in Malaysia in the form of small, hut-like structures. At the time, bamboo was therefore a "new" building material, which is ironic considering it is, in fact, one of the oldest. Even less commonplace were those workers with the necessary skills to put a relatively large bamboo structure together in accordance with our detailed drawings. The search for skilled workers led us to a team in Bandung in neighbouring Indonesia, who had been working on a range of bamboo structures in their homeland. They arrived on site after the foundations and concrete floor decks had been laid, and worked for about three months to fabricate the building.

Our way of working with the bamboo building team was highly collaborative, taking time to explain our intentions, understand their skills and respect their advice. It is common for working methods to change halfway through construction, and for design details to be rethought and redrawn to achieve the best results. Early discussions established the need to modify our more industrialised connections, which featured nuts and bolts, and modular metal fixings and clamps. In theory, these connections would enable us to build faster, but were significantly more expensive and beyond the team's expertise. The Bandung team were well versed in traditional friction joints and lashings, using simple, basic tools such as knives, saws and splitters,

so as a compromise it was decided to use techniques that were a cross between traditional and modern. For example, each column comprises five bamboo culms, which sit on protruding steel bars and have grouted cavities to create strong connections. The culms are then bolted and lashed to keep them together. We also fabricated custom three-pronged connector pipes to reinforce the corners of the four cantilevered treehouses (see figure 1, p 66).

The culms were treated in off-site workshops to enhance their service life, with batches delivered to the site and kept dry in temporary storage structures. Samples were then taken to a lab to test if they were properly cured, and any batches with negative results went through another round of treatment rather than being discarded. This practice saved time and costs, but also meant that the site transformed into a small treatment workshop and extra care had to be taken to ensure that any chemicals used were safely disposed of elsewhere.

Bamboo culms tend to crack easily. This occurs for various reasons, the main one being rapid expansion and shrinkage caused by exposure to sun and rain. To minimise this, the installed culms were covered temporarily with tarpaulin sheets as the building was being constructed. This protection was critical, especially when the woven mat ceiling was laid ahead of the roof covering. The mat is made from thin, narrow strips of bamboo, and deteriorates rapidly after exposure. Once all the culms and ceiling mats were in place, the roof covering, in the form of standing-seam aluminium decking, was put up immediately to protect the structure from rain.

Construction of the Bamboo Playhouse took almost three times as long as planned. The delay was due to the material being "new", and the fact that it required experimentation and research throughout the building process. Uncertainties about suitable bamboo species, and the need for strength testing and reprocessing of certain batches, set back the building work for months. In addition, finding an engineer to carry out structural calculations was a problem then, forcing the contractor to carry out time-consuming live load tests. Now there is more awareness of the sustainability of bamboo as a building material, these issues have become less acute.

Bamboo Classroom

LOCATION
Camarines Sur,
Bicol Peninsula,
Philippines

YEAR
2010

LATITUDE
13.7°N

THE BAMBOO CLASSROOM was built in 2010, two years after winning an international competition organised by MyShelter Foundation Philippines. Located in Camarines Sur in the Bicol Peninsula, the structure offers a prototype design for classrooms that could be built cheaply and replicated across the country.

The design adheres to the typical typology of linear classroom blocks found throughout South East Asia: one room deep with a veranda along the front. Our prototype comprises a pair of classrooms with bathrooms in between to limit the spread of noise, while the form of the building takes its cue from a typical vernacular domestic structure called the *bahay kubo*, or *nipa hut,* found all over the Philippine archipelago, which is characterised by the use of local materials such as bamboo, timber and nipah fronds, and tropical design forms such as large sloping roofs and shaded verandas. This simple arrangement allows for cross-ventilation and shading, which are vital in the hot, humid weather.

1

2

1 The Bamboo Classroom
2 Structural bamboo model

The classroom sits on an elevated concrete slab about 500mm above ground to keep flood waters at bay and protect the bamboo from ground moisture, which makes it susceptible to rot. A reinforced concrete frame sits on the slab and defines the classroom enclosure, to which bamboo culms are attached for the roof structure.

The connection between concrete and bamboo is simple: bamboo culms are lowered onto steel anchors cast earlier into the concrete frame and then secured by injecting screed mixture into the hollow of the pole, followed by bolting and lashing with strings. Elsewhere, bamboo-to-bamboo connections are made by running bolts through the culms, followed by more lashings.

The classrooms are simple rectangular enclosures with high ceilings and large wall openings filled with vertical culms. The roof consists of two mono-pitched planes over the entire building, arranged to create a clerestory between them at the highest point. The opening at the roof and the porous

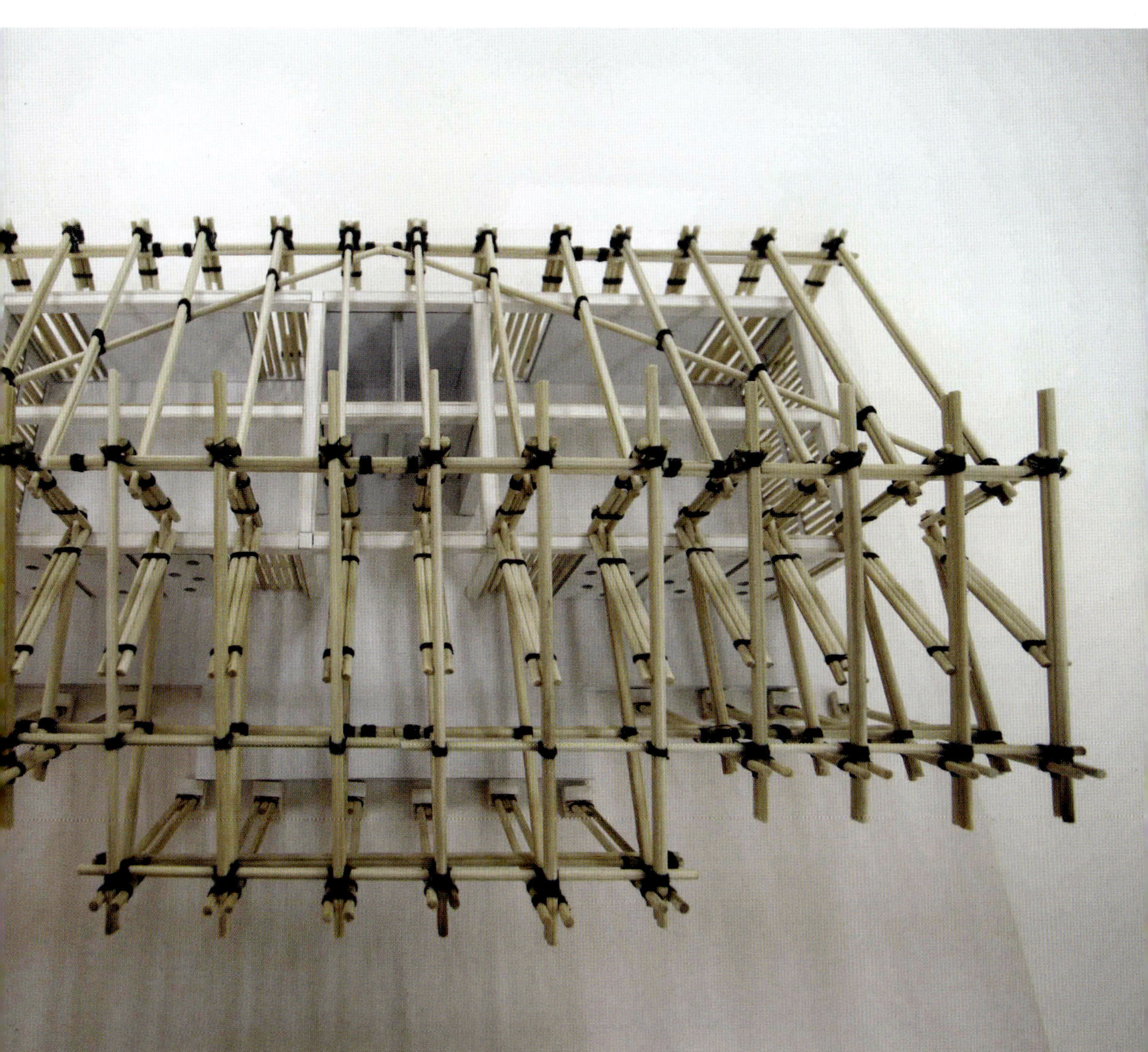

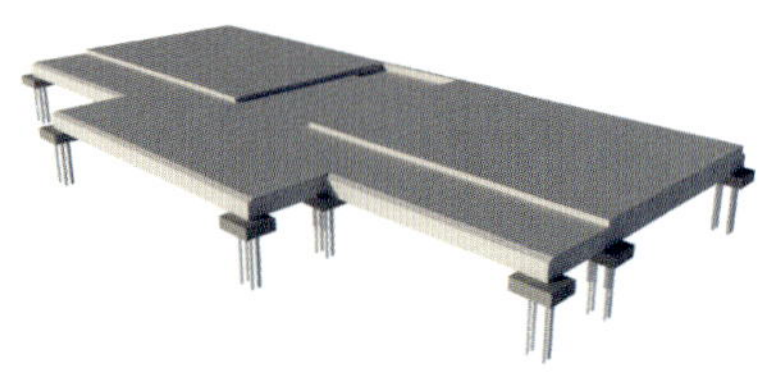
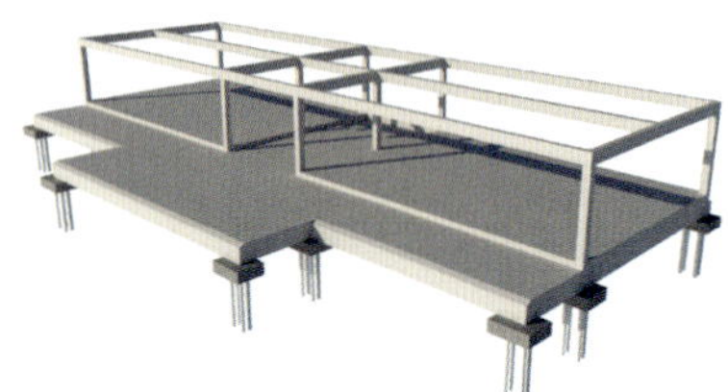
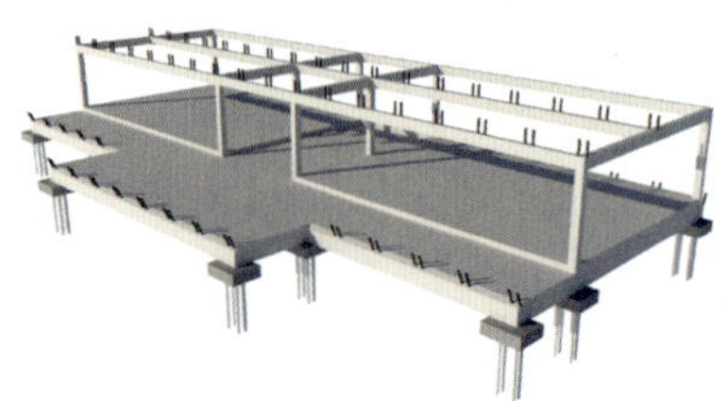
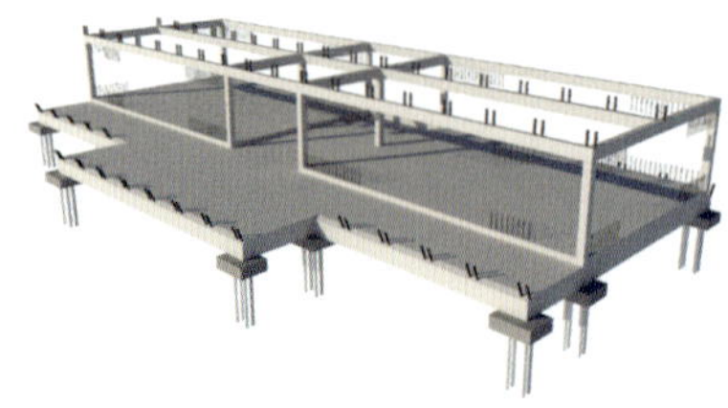
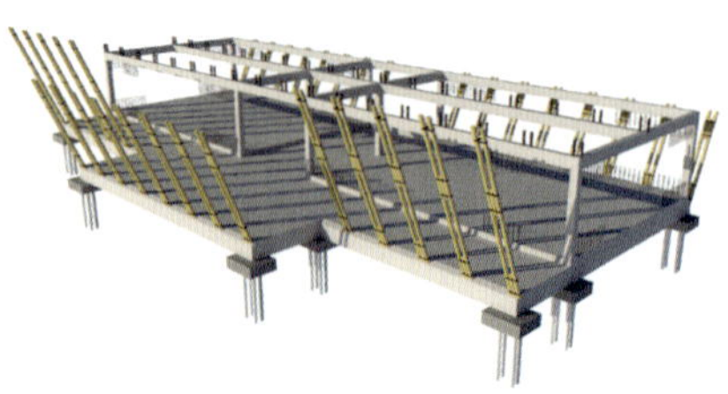
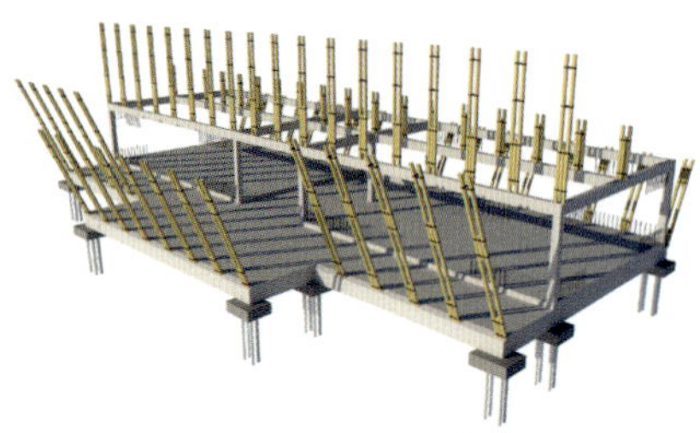
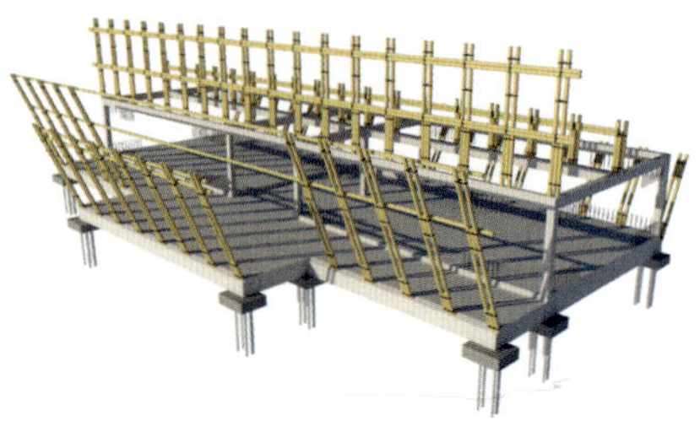

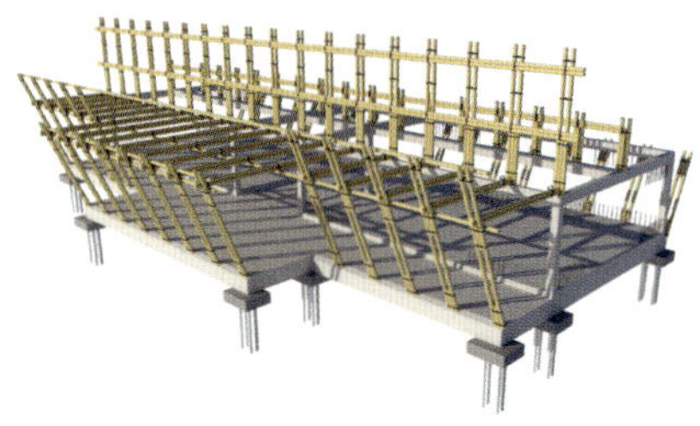
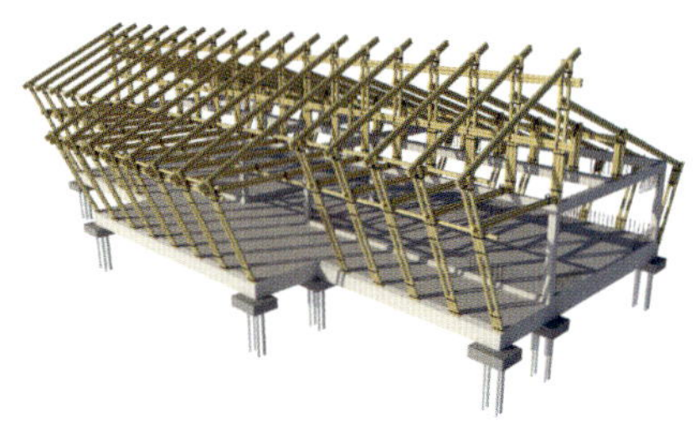
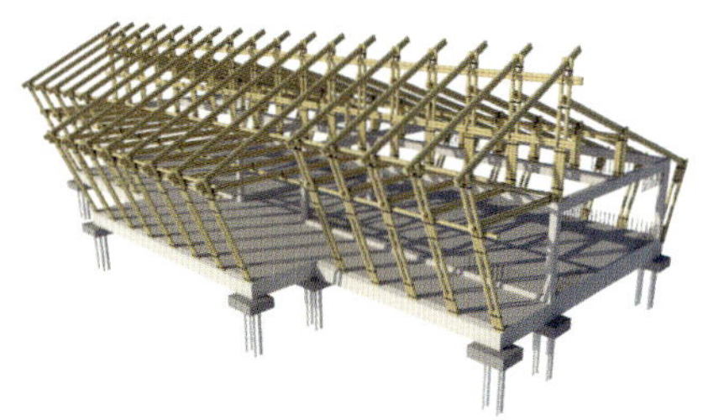
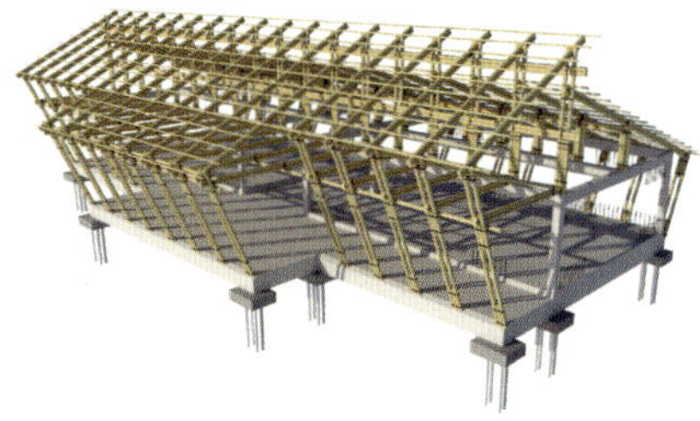
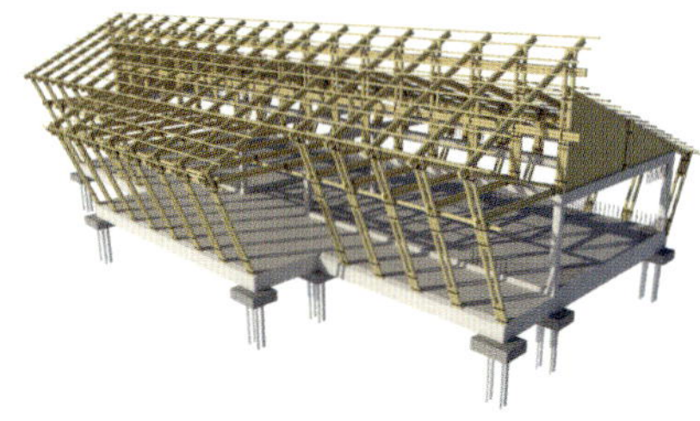
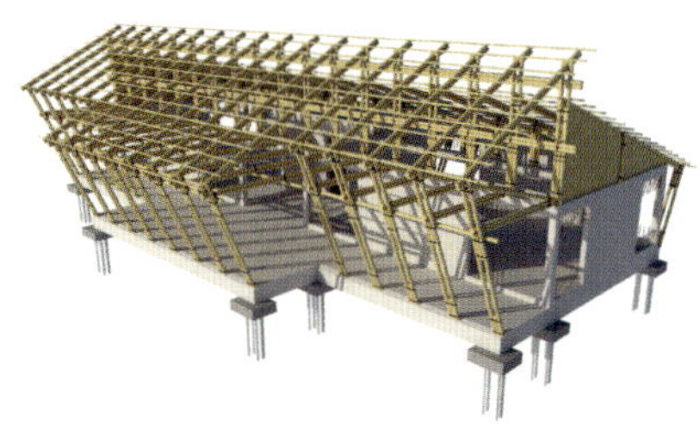
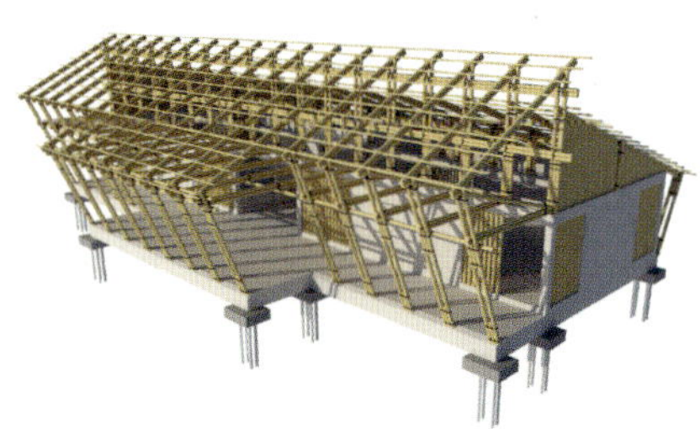
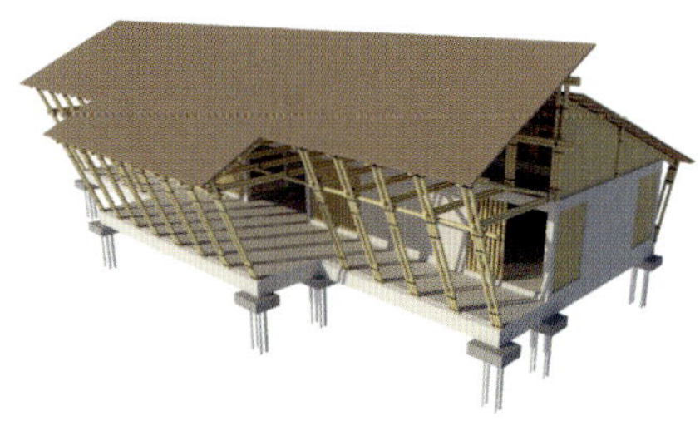

1

3

2

1 Children using the verandah as informal learning space

2 Classroom interior

3 Rear view of the Bamboo Classroom

wall work together to allow for cross-ventilation and warm air to escape at the top, keeping the classroom cool and comfortable. Outside the classrooms is a shaded veranda that widens at the centre to form an outdoor space for informal teaching and play. The ceiling here is lined with woven bamboo mats, originally used for making walls in vernacular dwellings.

When fully developed, the classroom blocks will be arranged linearly with 3-metre gaps between them and connected by the verandas, which provide a sheltered walkway between classrooms and the other school blocks. The verandas will face a central green space or playing field, allowing teachers to watch the children between classes.

The Garden Library

LOCATION
Perdana Botanical Gardens, Kuala Lumpur, Malaysia

YEAR
2020

LATITUDE
3.1°N

SITTING OPPOSITE THE Bamboo Playhouse which it complements, this small library plays with the imagery of a house and conveys a familiar, friendly appearance to encourage visitors. Closely placed vertical culms are tied together to form a three-dimensional house shape with a footprint of 1.2 metres x 2 metres, from which negative spaces are carved to create the entrance and bookshelves.

The whole structure is sheathed with a "raincoat" of colourful polycarbonate panels to protect the bamboo from weathering. On sunny days, these panels filter light between the culms, creating an interesting play of colours inside the library. The library contains mainly children's books, and it is not uncommon to find them being read inside the Playhouse's shaded spaces.

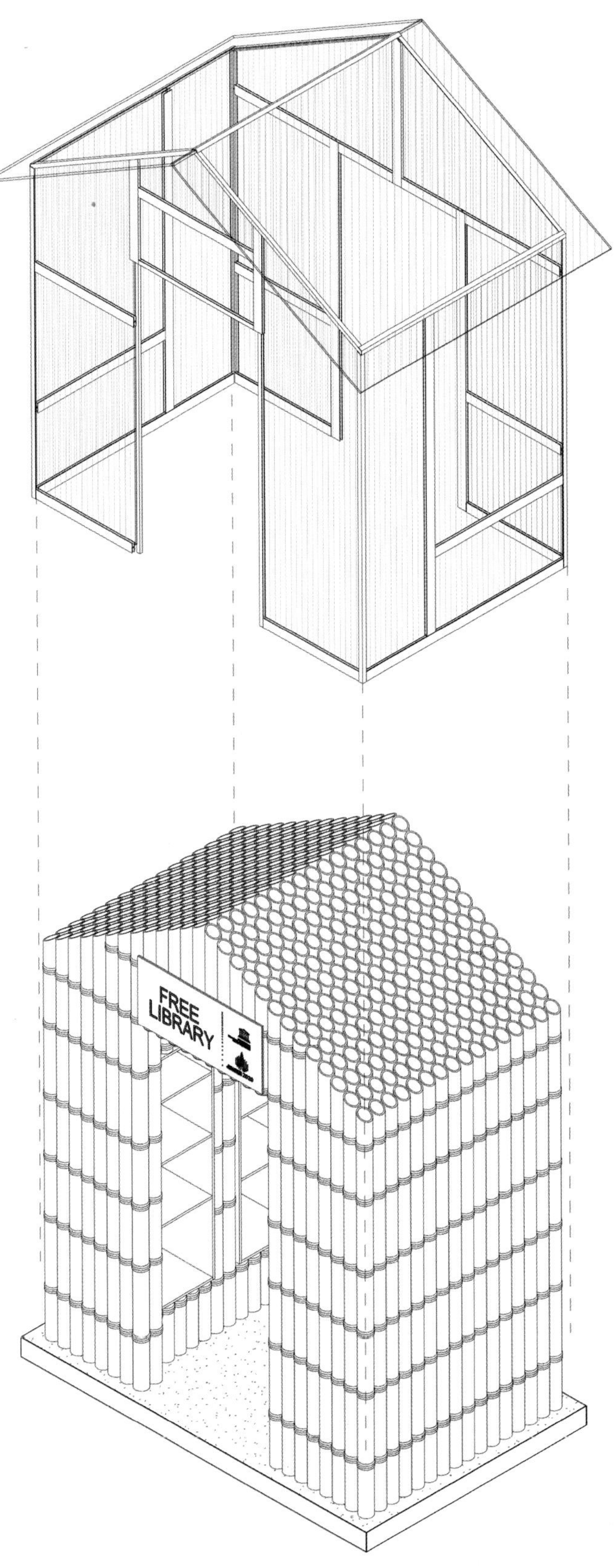

1 2

1 The little library being constructed by tying together vertical culms

2 The bamboo structure is sheathed with a "raincoat"

1

2

1 The library sits within the same area as the Bamboo Playhouse

2 Shelves are placed between vertical culms

ARCHITECTURE INSIDE + OUT
DIGITAL ARCHITECTURE
Herzog &

1 The library replicates the materiality of the bamboo playhouse

2 The ends of culms make the structure's soffit

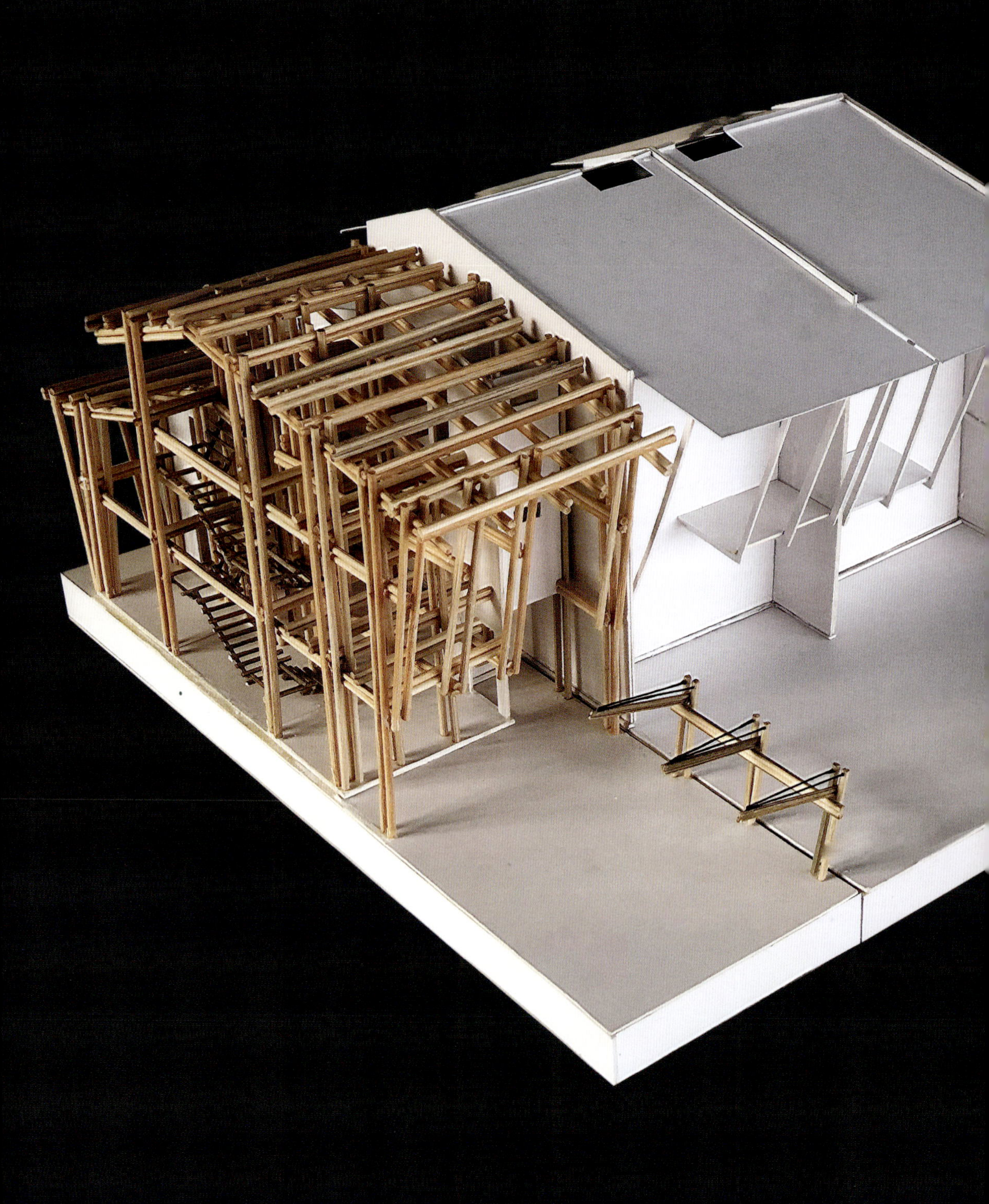

Bamboo Terrace Homes

LOCATION
Malaysia and regions where bamboo thrives

YEAR
2020

LATITUDE
–

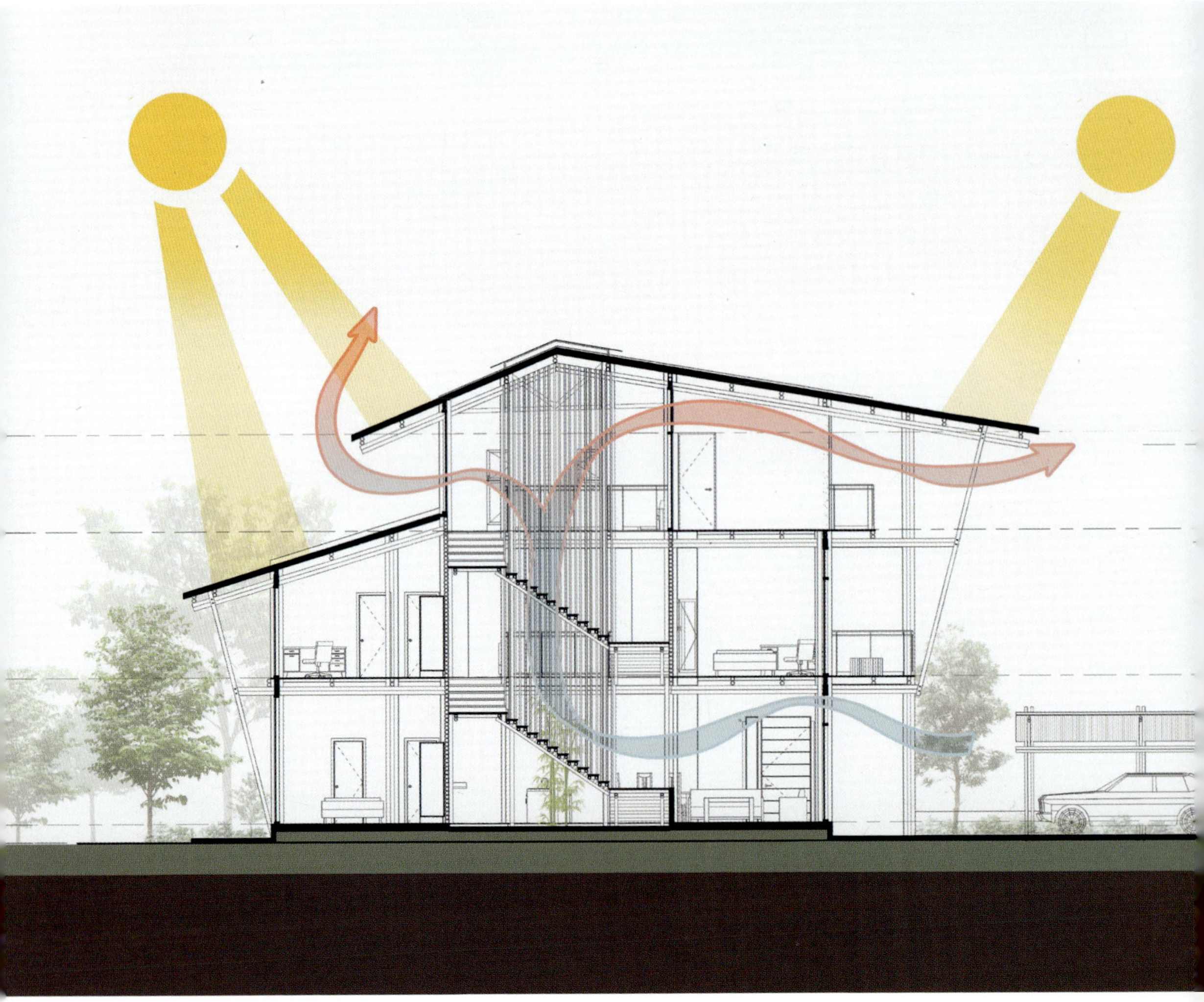

BAMBOO IS STILL considered an unusual building material, especially in its natural whole-culm form, and is commonly used for building types such as pavilions, rural structures and tourist developments. This proposal explores the use of bamboo in mass developments, specifically terraced housing. The idea here is to demonstrate that living in a home made from bamboo, widely regarded as a "poor man's timber", need not represent a regression in lifestyle (like living in a bamboo hut), and that a contemporary home with all modern comforts is entirely possible.

Using the proportions of a typical terrace house, a bamboo housing development could still be high density. Under this proposal, rows of terraces are designed to face streets for ease of access, while the backs look onto gardens to provide a safe environment for children to play. Externally, ground surfaces are kept as porous as possible, using permeable paving interspersed by strips of gardens planted with trees for shading.

Passive design strategies are used to deal with the hot and humid tropical climate and direct the architectural language. For example, angled bamboo columns supporting verandas and large roof overhangs work in tandem to provide shaded outdoor spaces and cut down solar gain inside.

1 Street view of the terrace homes
2 Open plan interiors encourage natural ventilation and large overhangs shade the house
3 Floor plans

1 2 3

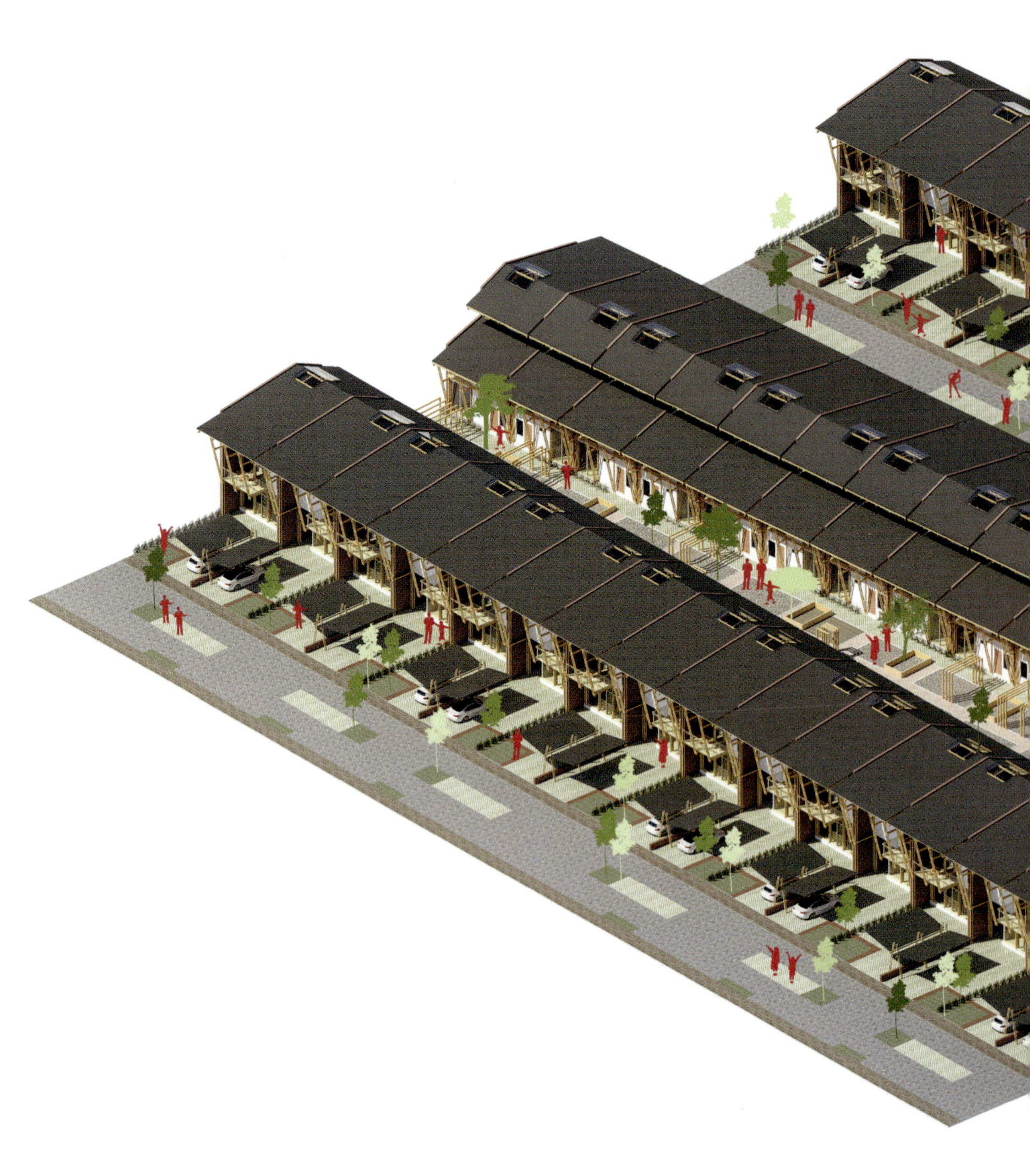

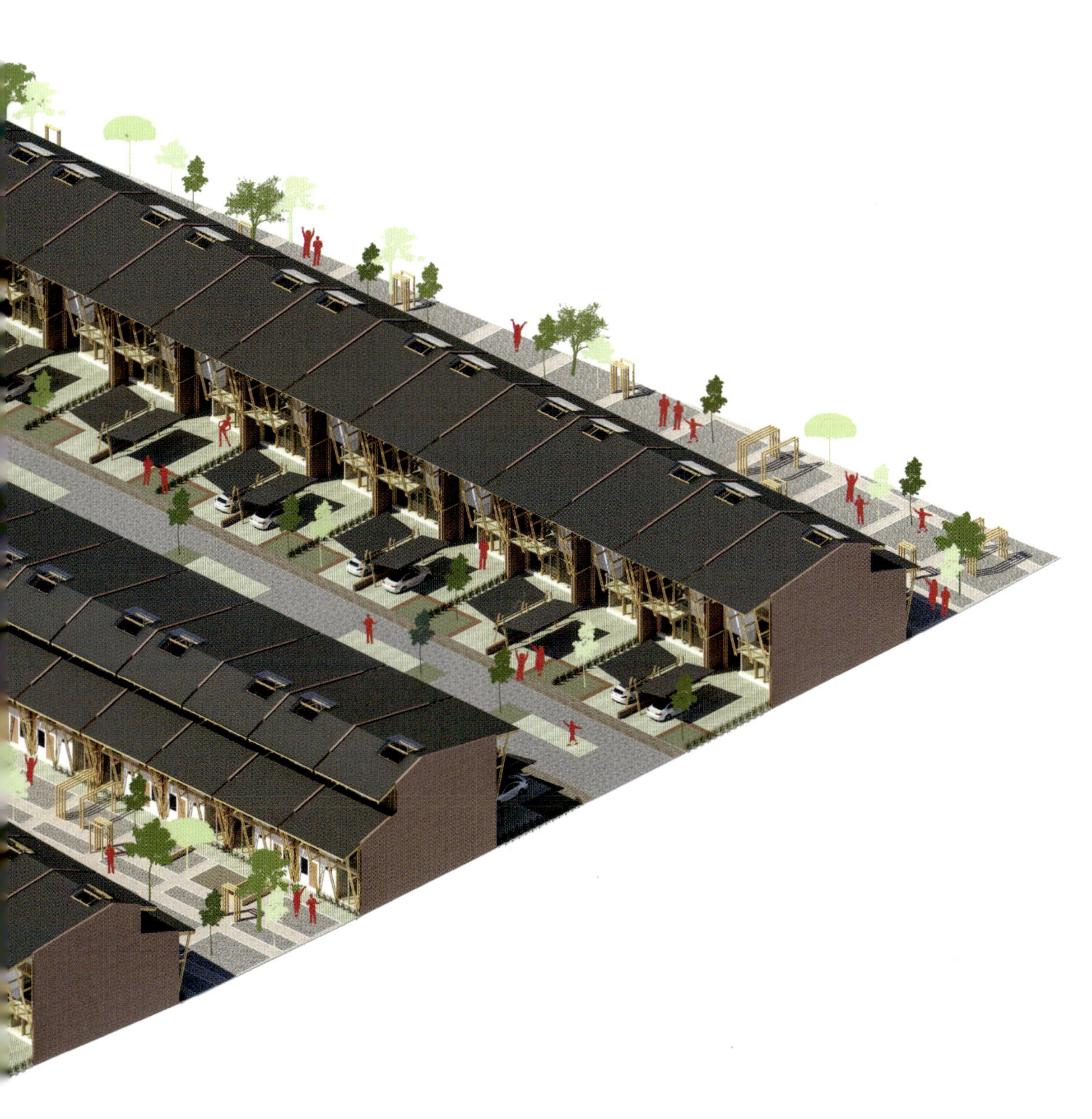

1

2

3

1–3 Images show that a contemporary lifestyle is possible with bamboo housing

An open ground-floor plan, fluid staircase voids and a small central courtyard garden enhance flexibility, creating horizontal and vertical connections between living spaces, as well as outdoor landscapes and views of the surrounding neighbourhood. This openness also encourages cross-ventilation and allows warm air to escape, while access to outdoor spaces is provided at different levels throughout the house via the ground-floor patio, first floor and attic verandas.

Developing this proposal without a client has given us greater freedom to explore the potential of bamboo in contemporary housing. However, a paper project is never entirely convincing for demonstrating the capacity to be built: bamboo is an incredibly challenging material and there are misgivings regarding its strength and durability. While we develop the finer design details, a prototype is currently planned to be built in partnership with a local university, to demonstrate the role bamboo might play in creating an alternative and more sustainable form of mass housing.

Typology and Environment

In several of their writings, the Smithsons discussed the concept of "conglomerate ordering" to describe the importance of inherent order in the existing fabric of a place:

"A characteristic of conglomerate order is its 'naturalness'; the feeling we experience of a fabric being ordered even when we do not understand it or are 'lost' ... We may not be able to see where we are, but can nevertheless navigate through our capacity to feel light and warmth and wind on our skins; sense of density of the surrounding fabric ..." [1]

The word "naturalness" suggests that the inherent order of a place guides our understanding of and response to it. For contemporary architects, the challenge is therefore to create order in a new building through a design that is natural and "without rhetoric". This implies a contextualist position where the conglomerate order of buildings shares a common language that ties them back to the overall urban fabric.

The idea that there is an inherent order in existing built forms is fundamental to our practice's climatic response in architecture, and, in this respect, typologies found within geographical territories where we design and build often become a starting point of reference. Aldo Rossi defines typology as "... a constant and manifests itself with a character of necessity; but even though it is predetermined, it reacts dialectically with technique, function, and style, as well as with both the collective character and the individual moment of the architectural artifact."[2]

Typologies contain within them the logic of form, and responses connected with reason and use, which create deep bonds with place and climate and allow us to start from a position of knowledge rather than from the beginning. From here, we can review solutions from the past and begin to analyse, dissect and improve designs based on contemporary concerns. Expanding on the importance of typology in environmental design, Dean Hawkes elucidated that "... the great value of typology, as opposed to singular types, in the production of new designs is that it constitutes a store of alternatives from which the starting point for the development of a promising solution might be drawn."[3]

This "store of alternatives" in typologies is constantly evolving as new developments in building and material technology, planning ideas, and physical, social and cultural contexts, emerge. However, this does not mean that typologies no longer being built are obsolete in terms of their design strategies. In fact, as Hawkes proposes, there may be good design potential for contemporary problems in earlier "stereotypes, particularly when modified with present-day technical developments".[4]

In view of this, we find ourselves less interested in modern building "types", where the tendency is to "exclude" climate with technology and energy-hungry mechanical solutions, than in those of the past which were driven by natural and passive systems. The former approach allows for the design of buildings in any form and orientation, and forgoes the need for large overhangs and shading devices; this results in effects of homogeneity and the loss of an architectural language distinctive to the tropics.

Opposite
Desa Mahkota school

Typologies that inform our work are those found within our local context, where environmental control is provided by natural ventilation, and lighting is, in large part, natural. With their low-carbon strategies, these structures, which include agrarian and early urban settlements, are becoming increasingly relevant today in addressing the climate crisis. Traditional Malay stilt houses, for example, were made from timber, bamboo and palm fronds, and were zero carbon in construction and operation, as they used circular economies to source renewable materials, and human energy sources rather than those based on fossil fuel. The typical Malay house is a detached pavilion-like structure with all its internal spaces one room deep, and is surrounded by coconut and fruit trees to provide shade. It also treads lightly on the ground and uses simple passive-design strategies, such as orientation, deep overhangs, verandas and strategically placed openings to permit airflow and cross-ventilation in response to the hot and humid tropical climate. Another climate-responsive typology found in this region is the Chinese shophouse, an early urban structure characterised by long, narrow plans arranged in terraces along main roads. These buildings are typically two storeys high, with commercial activities based on the ground floor in the front rooms, and the private living quarters located at the rear and upstairs. Multiple courtyards along their length admit daylight and air, and provide a private, shaded outdoor space. Offices, schools and institutions built during and just after the colonial period constitute other important typologies. Constructed of masonry, and long before air-conditioning became prevalent, they feature single-banked room layouts, high ceilings, and full-height openings fitted with timber shutters to control air flow and daylight levels, with verandas dotted along the outside walls to provide access and shading.

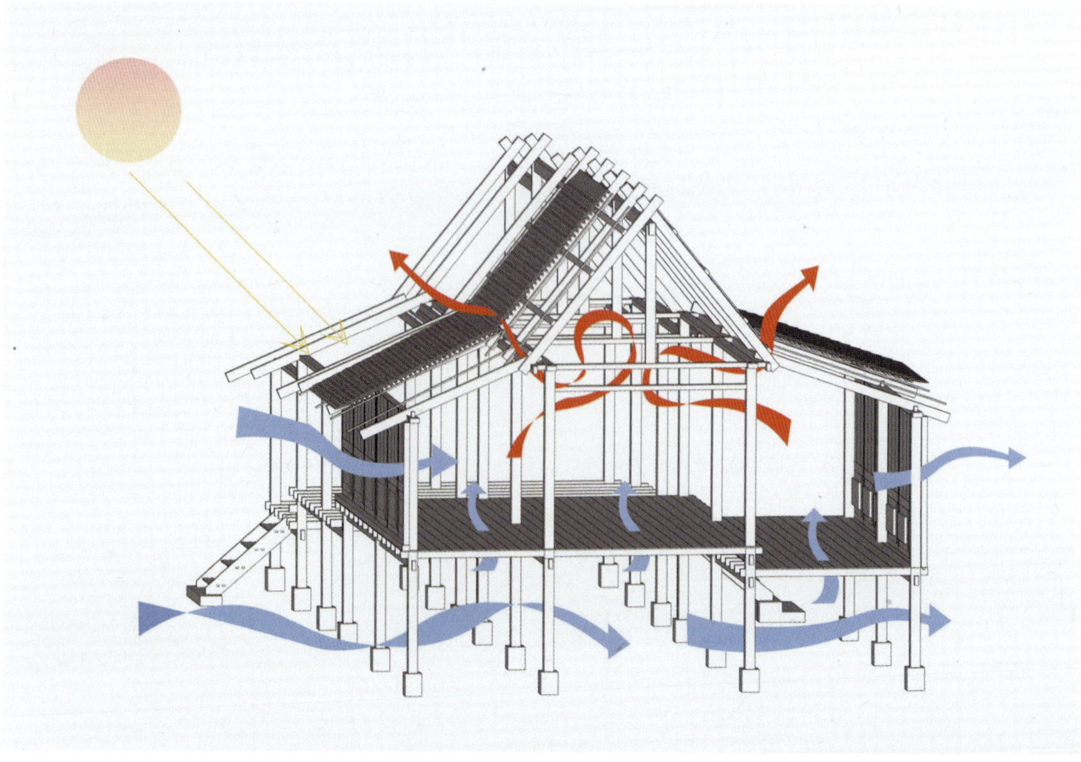

2

1

1 The environmental design of a Malay house

2 Desa Mahkota School site plan

PASSIVE STRATEGIES IN PRACTICE

Our work is characterised by being near the equator, where the climate is marked by intense sunlight, high temperatures and humidity. Given that most of the spaces we design are naturally ventilated, their environmental strategies focus on orientation and shading to reduce solar gain, and on removing warm air by encouraging air circulation. Near the equator, the sun's angle in the early morning and late afternoon is low, and hits east- and west-facing facades directly. It is thus essential to avoid these exposures, which can quickly lead to overheating. The sun's angle towards the north and south, on the other hand, is much higher and almost overhead, except at certain times of the year when it will dip slightly in the south. Thus, overhangs on the south facade will also help overcome heat gain.

The Desa Mahkota School, a 36-classroom secondary school in Kuala Lumpur completed in 2013, is an example where the climate is addressed through form and orientation rather than mechanical means. The standard school typology in Malaysia features long masonry blocks where classrooms with ribbon windows are arranged in single banks with open corridors to one side, which is an adaptation of the local vernacular layout of school buildings where spaces are one room deep with openings and verandas on both sides. The typological configuration, which can reach four storeys high, has changed little since it was first introduced in the 19th century and works exceptionally well in the tropical climate.[5] Fenestrations placed on opposite sides of the classrooms permit natural cross-ventilation and good daylight levels, while the corridors on the side offer access and shade. These features have been further improved in the Desa Mahkota School through additional passive environmental strategies, such as optimal orientation and shading devices.

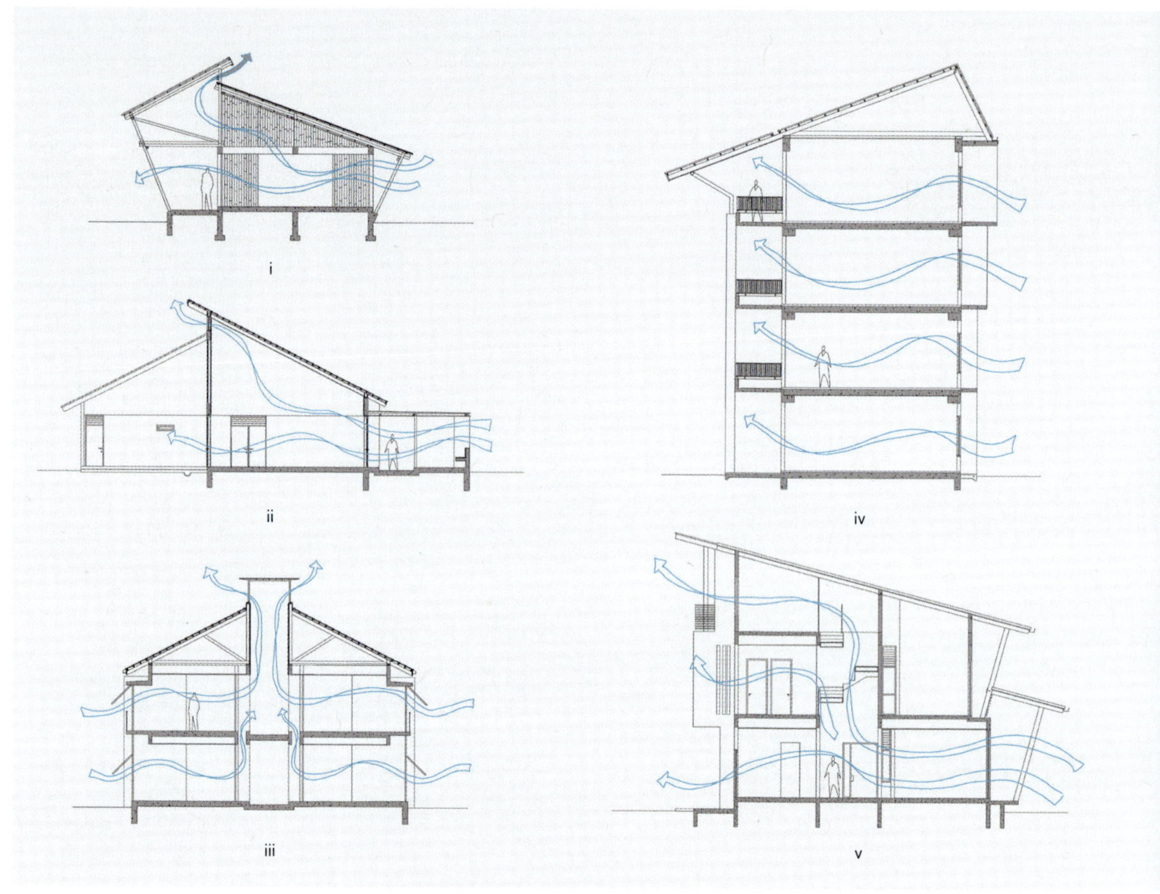

Like its predecessors, the Desa Mahkota School is composed of different-sized linear building blocks, each one room deep with a maximum depth of six metres, laid parallel to each other between courtyards, with their long axes lying east–west to avoid the direct morning and afternoon sun. This apparently simple layout conceals the fact that large volumes are being accommodated on a very tight urban site with no sense of overcrowding. The east–west orientation permits all the long facades to face either north or south, where the sun's rays are mostly overhead rather than facing and therefore easier to shade. The long corridors along the north facades are protected from rain by deep roof overhangs, while on the south side they are shaded from the midday sun – particularly necessary when the sun dips lower at certain times of the year – by both overhangs and masonry fins. A photograph of one of the south facades taken around midday shows these fins and overhangs doing precisely what they are meant to do: protecting the window openings and walls from direct solar gain and reducing glare (see figure p 106). The east- and west-facing facades, on the other hand, where the bathrooms and storage rooms are located, have few openings to minimise heat gain.

Approximately 85 per cent of the spaces in the school are therefore naturally ventilated, and mechanical systems, such as ceiling fans in classrooms and split-unit air-conditioning systems in teachers' and administrative rooms, are seen as secondary and used only as backup on particularly hot and humid days. Window openings are fixed with frosted glass louvres to permit airflow and a degree of privacy, while floor-to-ceiling heights are 3.6 metres, higher than those of a typical school, which further helps airflow. Other environmental design features include steeply pitched roofs to remove rainwater as quickly as possible, which, together with the surface rainwater collected from open drains, is channelled into a large underground tank to be filtered for reuse. The external grounds are landscaped with native trees and plants, except where hard surfaces are required for student assembly and vehicles; these are laid with porous paving to reduce flood risk and allow rainwater to percolate into the ground.

Hence, the significance of the Desa Mahkota School lies in its adaptation of a vernacular building form reconfigured to create learning spaces suitable for the tropical climate. As such, it demonstrates how a low-energy school can be achieved within the limits of modernist architecture by developing a full understanding of the local environment.

When warm air rises and gets trapped at the highest point in a building, it will affect overall comfort levels if not removed. Here, the process of removing warm air has been adapted from the vernacular device of steeply pitched roofs punctured by high-level openings, either at the gable ends or between roof sections. This aspect of our work is best understood by looking at the sectional studies of buildings. For example, a cross-section of the Bamboo Classroom in the Philippines, described earlier, illustrates how room-height openings covered with vertical bamboo screens work to draw fresh air into internal spaces and warm air out. At the same time, two mono-pitch roofs are angled to form a clerestory opening at the highest point, allowing warm air also to escape from the top. A similar strategy can be found in one of our earliest projects, the Rompin Hostel (2009) for young athletes in training, located in the small east-coast town of Rompin, South East Malaysia. Here, a covered outdoor terrace shades the large openings of the dining hall, which is a tall single-storey space under a large mono-pitch roof.

1 | 2

1 Natural flow of air through buildings in sections. i. Bamboo Classroom ii. dining hall, Rompin Hostel iii. dormitory block, Rompin Hostel iv. Desa Mahkota School v. Sepang House

2 Clerestory opening in the roof of the Bamboo Classroom

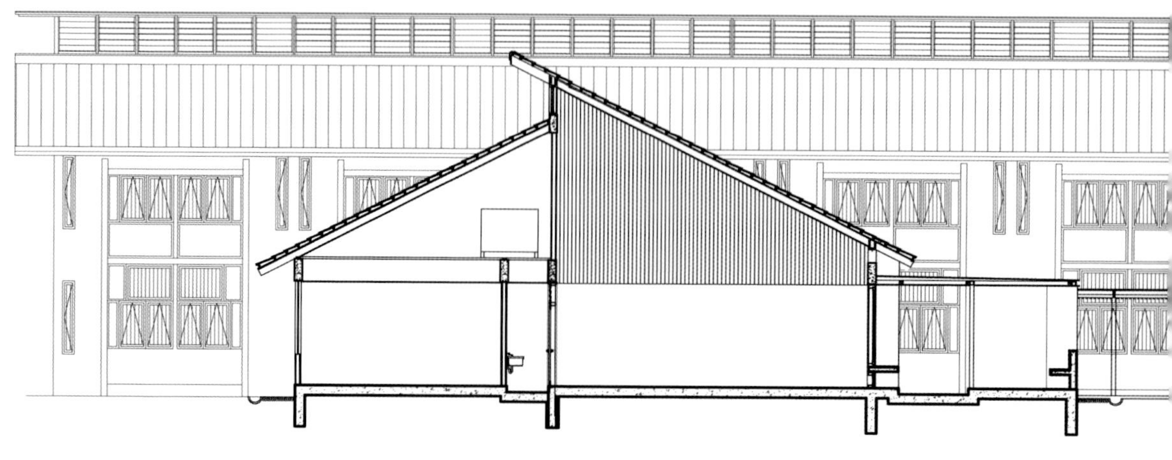

Dining hall

1 | 3
2 | 4

1 Rompin Hostel dining hall
2 Rompin Hostel site section
3 Rompin Hostel dormitory block
4 Rompin Hostel dormitory block sectional cutaway

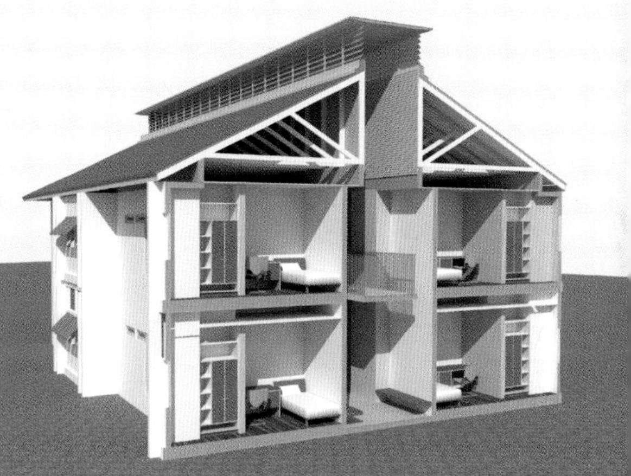

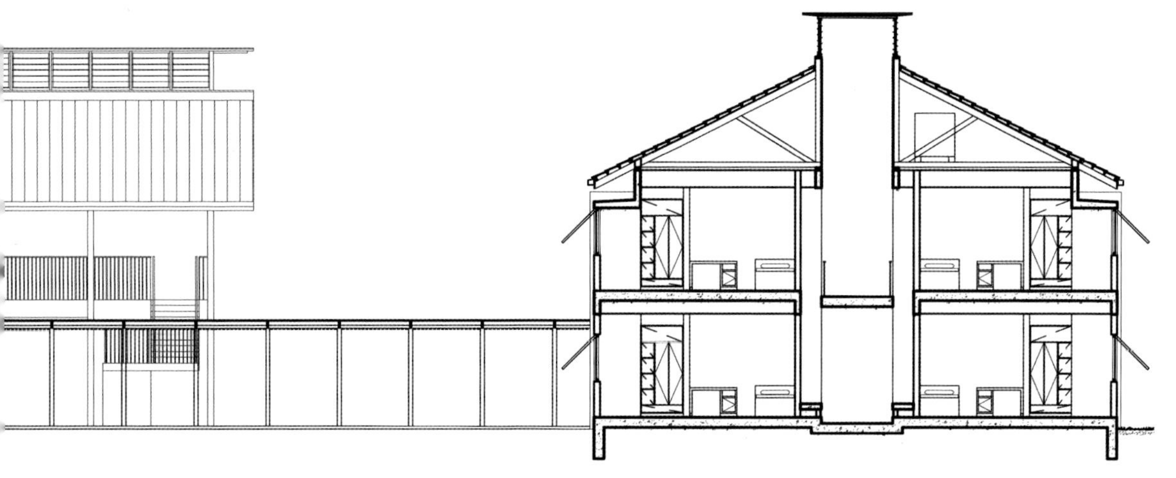

Dormitory block

Again, a sectional drawing of the space demonstrates how warm air rises and escapes through the clerestory at its highest point. The dormitory block, on the other hand, is two storeys high and contains bedrooms on either side of long corridors, an arrangement that can be difficult to ventilate naturally. In order to avoid any mechanical form of ventilation, the flat roof above the corridors is raised higher than the pitched roofs on either side, and clerestory openings with glass louvres are distributed along its length, permitting daylight to stream through and warm air to escape. In addition, openings are punched at intervals into the floors on the upper levels, to create stack ventilation. This system helps warm air rise from the ground and first floors to the top by means of a slight vacuum on the lower levels, and pulls fresh air through the bedroom windows.

With its steeply pitched roof with large overhangs designed to remove rainwater and direct it to an underground tank to be filtered and recycled, our Sepang House (2015), located about 40 kilometres south of Kuala Lumpur, also displays strong vernacular traits. The roof design allows for a large attic space, which acts as a temporary heat repository, collecting warm air and expelling it through wall openings by cross-ventilation. The success of this strategy is strengthened by the house's ground-floor open plan, where spaces flow into one another. This openness also extends vertically: double-height spaces and voids in the floor slabs make the house porous in both directions, facilitating airflow and ventilation.

The house plan is an arrangement of two parallel rectangular volumes laid east–west between a pair of spine brick walls, within which are the staircases and corridors. This composition means that the principal rooms – living room, dining room and kitchen – are situated on the north and south sides where they are shielded from direct early-morning and late-afternoon sun. As the sun is mostly overhead and less penetrating on these facades, they also feature more glazing, and are fitted with combinations of fixed glass, sliding doors and louvres. Glazing on the north facade is the largest as it faces the main garden and pool, so here the roof has a large overhang supported by closely spaced timber columns, with the shaded space beneath it functioning as a terrace with seating to enjoy the garden. Like the school project, openings on the east and west facades are much smaller, and are mainly recessed from the external walls to reduce solar gain. These external

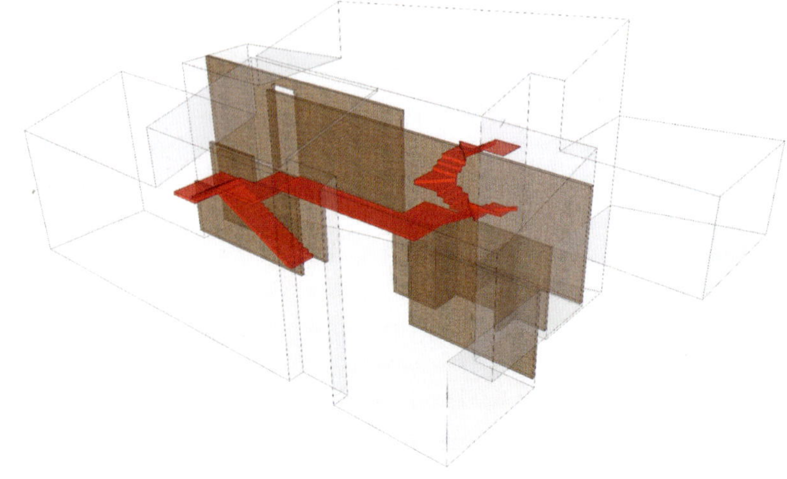

2

1

1 Two parallel rectangular volumes are laid east–west between spine brick walls in the Sepang House

2 Sloping roofs in the Sepang House

walls are made of exposed concrete and have substantial thermal mass. Shaded by large roof overhangs and tall trees, the walls stay cool for most of the day and help to regulate the temperature in the house.

DESIGNING FOR THE TROPICS

The shape and form of our buildings are produced in direct response to the climate and apply passive strategies used in existing and historical typologies, adapted to suit current methods of construction. This approach reflects an attempt to ground our work in the understanding that modernist architecture, developed largely in temperate countries, may not be suitable for transplantation elsewhere in the world without taking into account local climate and context. The ubiquity of modernist building types in the tropics is closely related to the extensive use of air-conditioning to create comfortable living and working conditions, a practice that has led to widespread environmental degradation. Understanding local and regional typologies, and how they have developed over time, has therefore helped ease the challenge of defining a contemporary architectural idiom for this part of the world.

ENDNOTES

1. The phrase "conglomerate ordering" came about during Alison and Peter Smithson's teaching at the University of Bath from 1978 to 1990, and their parallel involvement with ILAUD (International Laboratory of Architecture and Urban Design) from 1978. It first appeared in print in "On the Edge", an essay they published in the ILAUD Yearbook 1984/85, which was closely followed by "Conglomerate Ordering", published in the ILAUD Yearbook 1986/87.
2. Rossi, Aldo, *The Architecture of the City*, Diane Ghirardo and Joan Ockman trans, Cambridge, MA: MIT Press, 1982, p 41.
3. Hawkes, Dean, Jane McDonald and Koen Steemers, *The Selective Environment*, London, UK: Taylor & Francis, 2002, p 47.
4. Hawkes, Dean, *The Environmental Tradition: Studies in the Architecture of Environment*, London, UK: E & FN Spon, 1996, p 55.
5. Some of the earliest schools in Malaysia, such as Penang Free School (established 1816), Malacca High School (established 1826) and St Thomas' Secondary School, Kuching (established 1848), were built by the British during the colonial period and in the early 20th century evolved to become a standard design, characterised by single-bank linear blocks lined with corridors on one side.

Desa Mahkota School

LOCATION
Desa Parkcity,
Kuala Lumpur,
Malaysia

YEAR
2013

LATITUDE
3.2°N

THIS IS A GOVERNMENT-FUNDED secondary school designed to serve an urban neighbourhood in the north-west part of Kuala Lumpur city. With a capacity to accommodate up to 1,200 students and 60 teaching staff, the school boasts 36 classrooms, multipurpose halls, laboratories, a library, a canteen and administration rooms.

The site on which the building sits is tight, having to accommodate 11,000 square metres of teaching space within 1.8 hectares of land. Spaces are arranged in parallel linear blocks ranging from two to seven storeys high along the east–west axis, with narrow courtyards in between. The trees in the courtyards play a major role in providing shade and cool to the buildings during the day, which will be enhanced when they are fully mature. The courtyards also soften the angular geometry of the building blocks, making them feel less institutional.

1 Spaces are arranged in parallel linear blocks with courtyards in between

2 Fins and overhangs on the south facade

1

2

1 Section through the academic blocks
2 A narrow courtyard between teaching blocks
3 Ground floor spaces are fluid open spaces to cater for different activities
4 Bright-coloured paint is used to identify each block
5 Classroom space

5

All teaching spaces are accessible from corridors lining the north faces of the blocks, while the south facades are fitted with fins and overhangs that shade window openings, creating consistency of design across the whole development. Specific colours – used on the staircases and south facades of each block – help staff and students navigate their way round the building. Many of the ground floor spaces between columns are fluid, without walls or partitions, and function a bit like those under a traditional house raised on stilts, so can be used for different activities. In the school, these become a continuous open space linking the main hall and canteen, and are closely connected to the green courtyards. Students regularly gather and socialise in this space between classes, which is also used for co-curricular activities that sometimes spill into the courtyards.

Sepang House

LOCATION
Sepang, Selangor,
Malaysia

YEAR
2015

LATITUDE
2.9°N

THIS RESIDENTIAL HOUSE sits on a rather unremarkable 950 square-metre plot of land that is flat and barren, and surrounded by other identical plots, most of which are currently vacant. Nearby is a large man-made lake (developed when Putrajaya, Malaysia's administrative city, was built in the late 1990s), which is visible only from the roofs of the surrounding houses. As there were no real views, it felt important to create one within the small plot, and to achieve this the house's footprint was aligned close to the southern boundary, leaving space for a generous garden and swimming pool on the north side. The principal rooms, such as the living and dining rooms, kitchen, and master and guest bedrooms, all have views onto the garden, which is now adorned with large mature trees. A terrace – shaded by a large roof overhang and the trees –

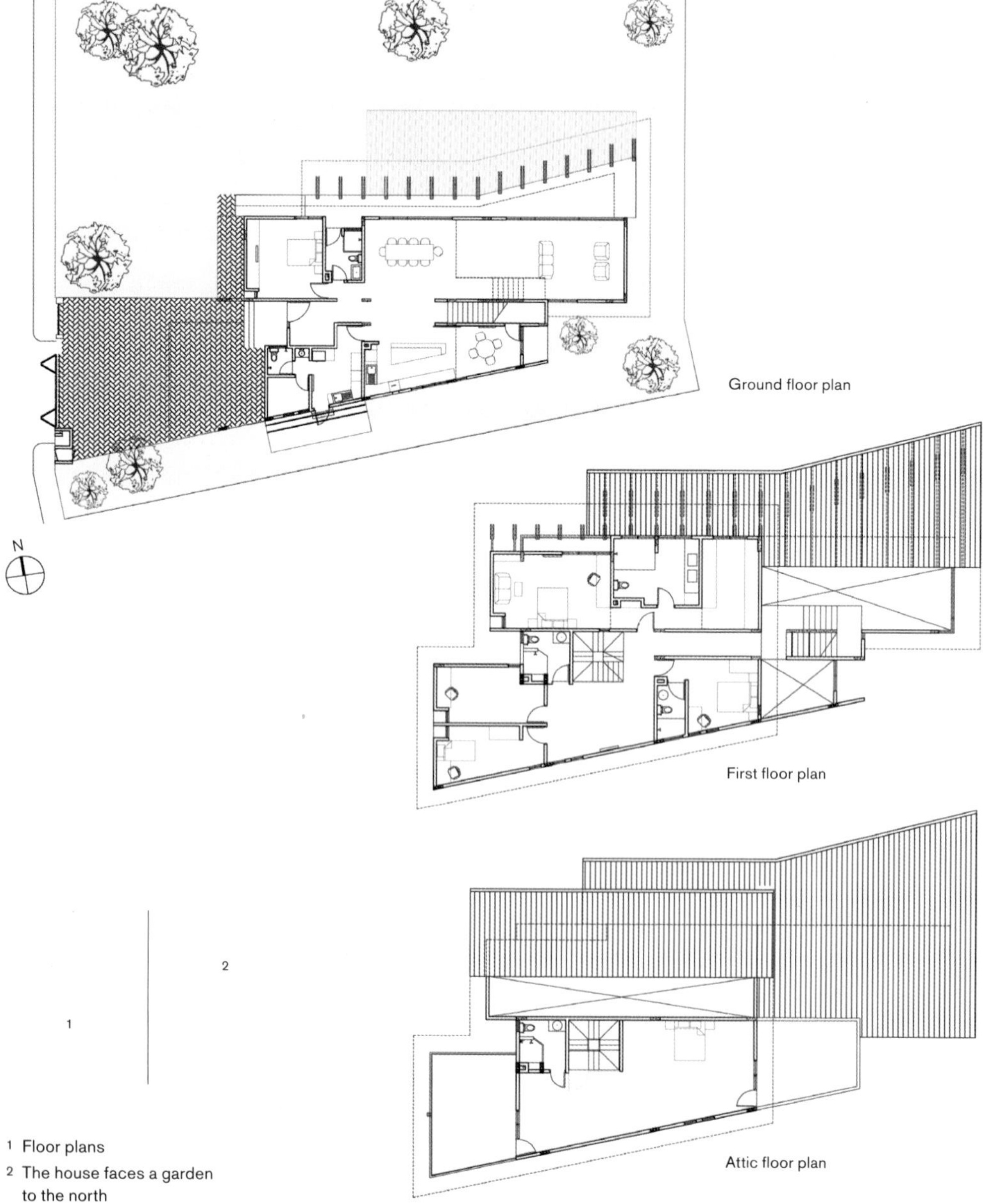

1 Floor plans
2 The house faces a garden to the north

runs along the north side and becomes an intermediary space between the inside and outside.

External walls are finished in bare concrete, whose coldness belies the warmth of the interior spaces: floors and ceilings – the latter set directly under the pitched roof – are timber, while all the internal walls are either exposed brickwork or plastered and painted white. This combination of several different materials creates textural richness, as well as changing effects of light and ambience as one moves through the house, providing a varied background for daily family life.

There are three levels to the house: the ground floor has an open layout to encourage family interaction, while the middle floor contains the bedrooms; the highest level is the attic, a single large space under a steeply pitched roof, which functions as a home office and gym and offers views of the Putrajaya Lake.

1 Brick walls line the double height spaces in the house
2 Folded steel staircase links the first floor to the attic space
3 Interior spaces are generally open, bright and airy
4 The attic space

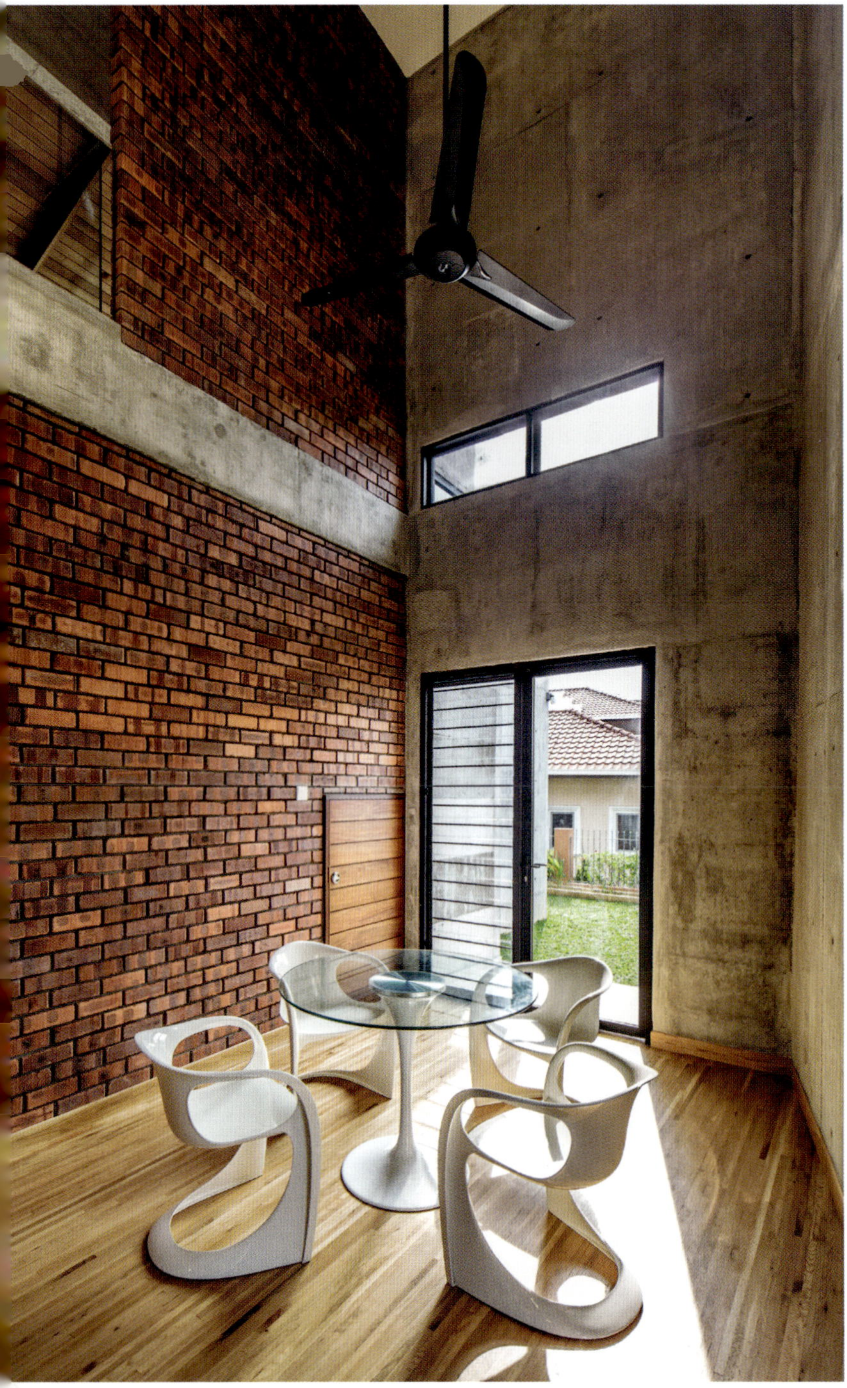

The Outdoor Room

The concept of an outdoor room, a private zone surrounded by internal space but open to the sky, has profound significance for how we think about dwellings. Having a piece of open space that is entirely one's own, to do with as one wishes, and that also brings in light and air, and sometimes wind and rain, is very much about establishing a relationship with a specific place, and with nature and the cosmos. The outdoor room was used in one of my earliest independent works, where a terrace house was reimagined for the Welsh House of the Future competition, in 1999. The shortlisted scheme – a home in the Welsh valleys – comprised a small courtyard inserted at the centre of a two-storey narrow building, with all internal spaces looking directly onto it, and a ground floor that also extended out to it, establishing a close relationship between the inside and outside.

"The dwelling, if it is for a family, must be in immediate contact with nature … Just as there must be a hierarchy of man-made domains in the city, so, too, the enjoyment of nature demands its own hierarchy of scale and subdivision, ranging from the great natural landscape to the tiny cultivated outdoor room of one's own."[1]

As this quotation from Serge Chermayeff and Christopher Alexander's book *Community and Privacy: Toward a New Architecture of Humanism* suggests, the "outdoor room" can play an essential role in the design of a home, and should be arranged as a series of hierarchies similar to city planning. Chermayeff and Alexander believed that mass technology and the densification of post-war cities had led to a loss of community and privacy. Recognising the need for an outdoor room, in the late 1950s and early '60s, Chermayeff, along with students at Harvard University, developed Patio Houses, which featured outdoor spaces or courtyards divided between rooms and

1 | 2

1 End-lot House with wall openings to the roof garden
2 Welsh House of the Future

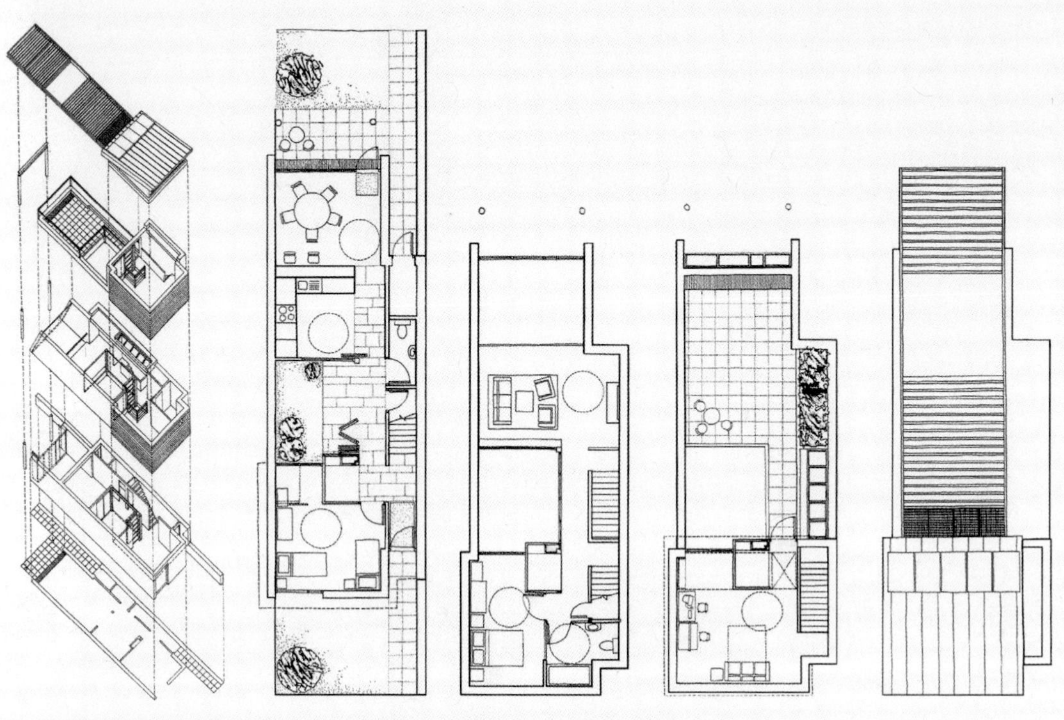

enclosed by walls, providing multiple pocket gardens. Each patio was explicitly related to an indoor function and domain occupied by adults, children and family, while lobbies or "locks" were used to separate the different zones. This extreme form of compartmentalisation emphasised the importance Chermayeff attached to privacy: "… every dwelling must contain an acoustic hierarchy, closely linked to the enjoyment of sun, air, and light, so that even in the outdoor room of one's own, the smallest desired sound can be heard and enjoyed."[2]

Chermayeff's own patio house in New Haven, built in 1962–63, has three cells linked by narrow corridors.[3] The rooms are shallow in plan and have windows on opposite sides of the wall, meaning that cross-ventilation can occur naturally, while courtyards create pleasant extensions to the living space. Here, parents can entertain guests in the first courtyard, away from the children's rooms and their attached patio.

In Fredensborg, Denmark, Jorn Utzon similarly created highly liveable homes using L-shaped plans where the focus of the interior space was the courtyard. Forty-seven home units were designed as serrated terraces, each one turning its back to the street but opening up fully to the courtyard. The facades facing the street are built like a fortress: windows are fitted with metal bars, and walls are high and kept at arm's length from the street by trimmed beech hedges. In contrast, the facade that faces the courtyard is fitted along its length with full-height glass, blurring the boundaries between inside and outside. The workshop or hobby room, which is directly accessed from the courtyard, further reinforces the latter's role as an extension of the living areas. Utzon made clear his intentions when he wrote that "… within their own area people could do as they pleased in

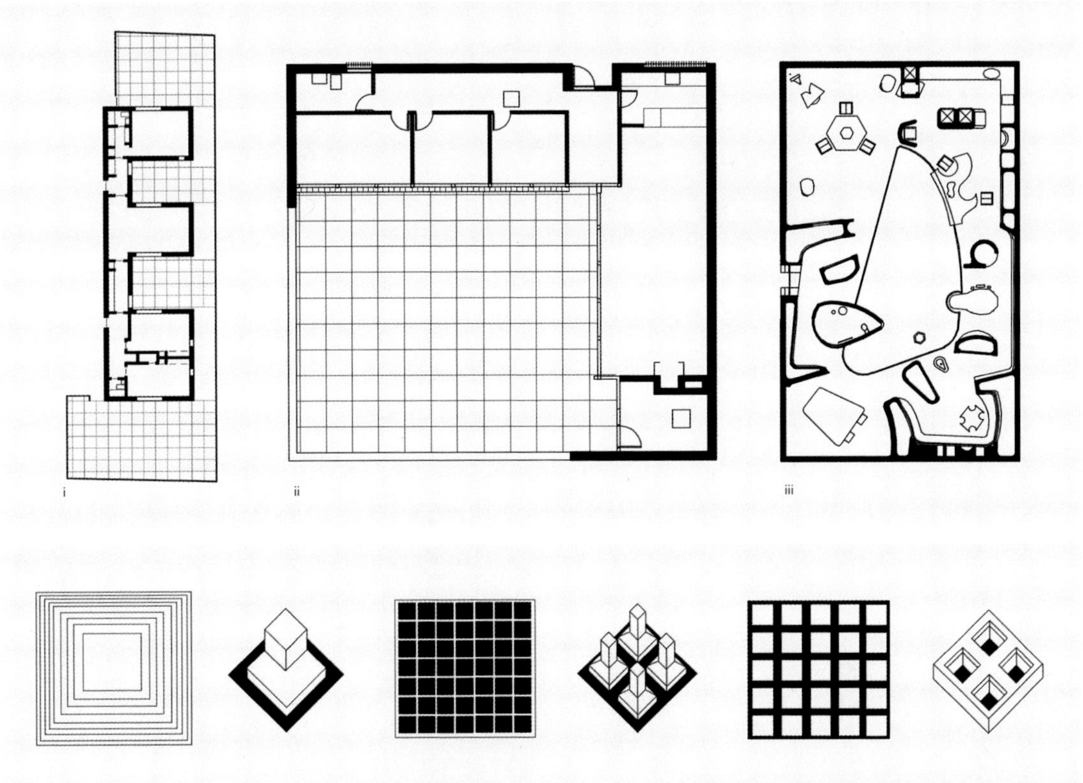

1 Welsh House of the Future

2 i New Haven Patio House
ii Fredensborg Courtyard House
iii House of the Future for Daily Mail Ideal Home Exhibition 1956

3 Fresnel Diagram and density studies of the pavilion and court form

their leisure time without upsetting their neighbours, and without having any special easements ..."[4]

From the outset, Utzon had intended the houses to be more like a village than a housing estate, and to cover an area large enough to form a landscape. Similar to Chermayeff's patio houses, a massive tract of land was required for their development, which may not be feasible in all contexts. The opportunity to enjoy outdoor activities in private seems to come with a high cost, but there is also evidence to the contrary. The relationship between density and form was analysed in the 1970s by Leslie Martin and Lionel March, who found the courtyard performed best in terms of efficiency of coverage and daylight levels when compared with forms such as pavilions and linear blocks: "The court form is seen to place the same amount of floor space on the same site area with the same condition of building depth and approximately one-third the height required by the pavilion form."[5]

Their theory originated from Raymond Unwin's recognition that "the area of a circle is increased not in direct proportion to the distance to be travelled from the centre to the circumference, but in proportion to the square of that distance".[6] This was demonstrated by the concentric squares in the Fresnel Diagram, in which the area of successive outer bands is the same as the central square, thus demonstrating the effectiveness of distributing a building's footprint up to the perimeter of a site instead of confining it to the centre.

In a similar vein, Alison and Peter Smithson advocated homes in high densities with their House of the Future designed for the Daily Mail Ideal Home exhibition in London, in 1956.[7] Conceived in response to future conditions, the house had moulded cave-like spaces that looked into a central outdoor courtyard, which they described as a "vertical tube of unbreathed private air",[8] and an unpierced skin around the whole exterior, save for the main entrance door. The result was a highly introverted and private house, which, when grouped tightly together with others, could achieve a density of up to 80 homes per acre. Inside, the courtyard acted as the central focus, as each room opened on to it, and was designed as an oasis with wild grass, flowers and trees. In one corner, rainwater from the roof was directed to a highly contrived waterspout, which cranked down implausibly from roof level and expelled water into a plastic hopper for birds. This celebration of nature in the courtyard provided a strong contrast to the highly synthetic interior, where everything – chairs, tables, kitchen cabinets, partitions, curtains and even bed sheets – was specified by the Smithsons as made of nylon.

Courtyard houses provide their occupants with an outdoor space for leisure activities and children's play that offers greater privacy than a back garden. Their introspective character also permits houses to be grouped closely together, increasing urban density and maximising land use. From the early years, we have opted repeatedly for this format in our projects, using U- and L-shaped plans bounded by pavilions and garden walls.

THE TROPICAL COURTYARD HOUSE

The courtyard house form is present in many regions of the world that are geographically, climatically and culturally distinct. The projects described above in Northern Europe and America raise universal issues concerning outdoor rooms, but the climatic and cultural conditions in which they are situated are very different from those that prevail in the tropics. The typical urban courtyard house in South East Asia – the Chinese merchant's "shophouse", with its long volumes and narrow frontage facing a street or canal, which resulted from urban planning restrictions imposed by British colonial rule – originated in China, along with its entrepreneurs, at a time when European trading posts were being established in Indochina and the Malay Archipelago.[9] This Chinese typology is known as *siheyuan* in Beijing, meaning "quadrangle", and refers to an unadorned single-storey building surrounded by high walls, with one or more internal courtyards or lightwells, housing three or four generations. The inner courtyards provide shelter from the noise and dust of the street, and cold north winds, while allowing the sun to penetrate. When transported to the South East Asian tropics, this Chinese domestic model transforms into a colonial shophouse fitted with open ventilation grills in partitions and walls, and doors and windows around the courtyards covered with louvred shutters, to encourage natural ventilation throughout the building.

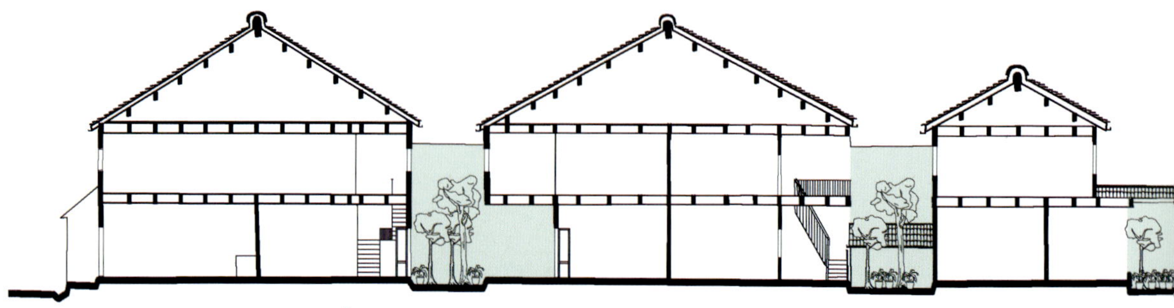

1 Section through Chinese shophouse
2 Ventilation louvres in a Chinese shophouse
3 Chinese shophouse courtyard

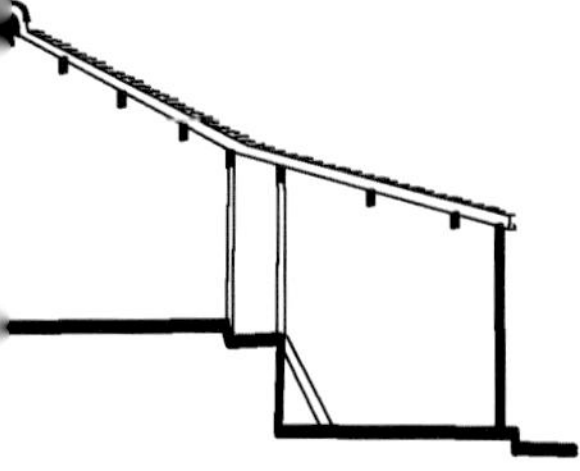

The design of the shophouse can act as a model for urban housing. An early research project carried out in 2007 gave us the opportunity to explore how a tropical terrace house could be improved by introducing an internal courtyard without affecting the densities of large groupings. The typical house's narrow frontage and deep plan allow it to be grouped closely together with others but can also result in dark and stifling interiors. This type of house also offers very little privacy where overlooking is a problem, particularly for rooms facing neighbouring houses across narrow back lanes. There have been attempts to overcome these issues by introducing small light wells within the deep plan, but these often end up being blocked off by occupants to keep out the rain.

The project began with the typical 22 x 75 ft terrace house, creating a total built area of 184 square metres spread over two floors, and a floor-to-ceiling height of 2.7 metres. By varying the building footprint proportions and courtyard sizes, it was possible to construct several viable courtyard house plans (see figure 1, below). For each plan variation, simple investigation methods were used, including calculations of the exposed wall-to-volume ratio, maximum room depth between openings, and sun and shadow projections, followed by a critical appraisal of internal planning potentials. Here, the measure of good environmental design criteria was based on Victor Olgyay's well-known taxonomy of environmentally determined building forms, which recommended that an elongated rectangular building shape – that is, a shallow plan with large, exposed surfaces, and long walls facing north and south – is best in a hot, humid climate.[10] From this study, it was possible to develop a courtyard house for the tropics that offered good environmental design, with wide frontage to make the street feel less crowded, and a generous outdoor room within the confines of the home, without adversely affecting densities when grouped back-to-back in rows of terraces.

Working with slightly lower densities, the Vermani house is an existing semi-detached house that has been remodelled and extended. Located in Kuala Lumpur and completed in 2014, it was designed to accommodate a young couple's growing family with a new extension added to the rear, separated by a small circular courtyard and a terrace on the ground and first floors, respectively. These outdoor spaces serve as intermediaries between the public zone of the house – the living room, dining room, kitchen, and rooms for visiting guests – and the quieter, private zone to the rear, containing the

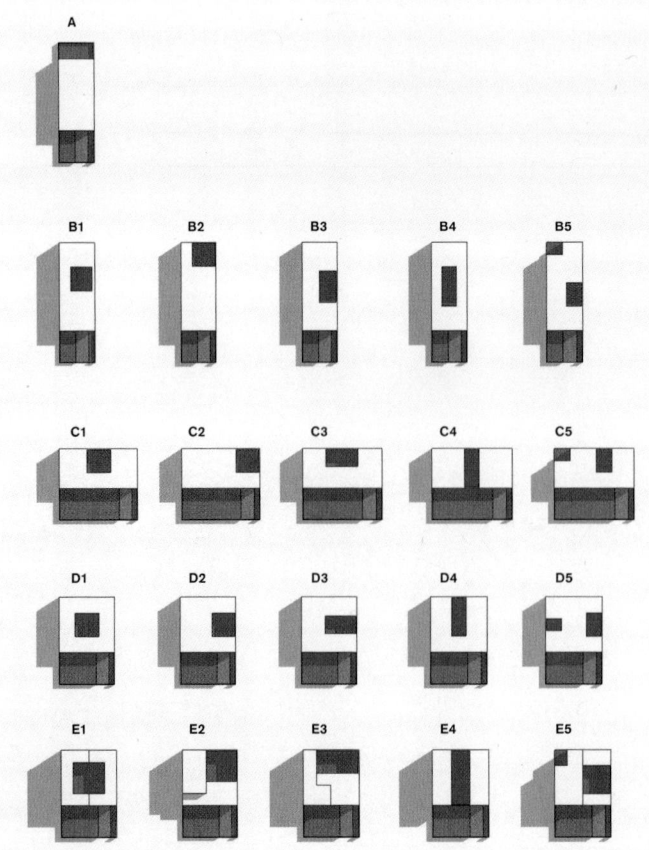

Typical terrace layout
2 storeys
Plot dimension 6.7x22.9m (22'x75')
Building footprint area 92m²
Total built up area 184m²
Total backyard footprint 20.4m²
Total courtyard footprint 0m²
6m setback along the front

Courtyard terrace B
2 storeys
Plot dimension 6.7x22.9m (22'x75')
Building footprint area 112m²
Total built up area 184m²
Total backyard footprint 0m²
Total courtyard footprint 20.4m²
6m setback along the front

Courtyard terrace C
2 storeys
Plot dimension 15x13.6m
Building footprint area 112m²
Total built up area 184m²
Total backyard footprint 0m²
Total courtyard footprint 20.4m²
6m setback along the front

Courtyard terrace D
2 storeys
Plot dimension 10.6x16.7m
Building footprint area 112m²
Total built up area 184m²
Total backyard footprint 0m²
Total courtyard footprint 20.4m²
6m setback along the front

Courtyard terrace E
2 & 1/2 storeys
Plot dimension 10.6x16.7m
Building footprint area 112m²
Total built up area 184m²
Total backyard footprint 0m²
Total courtyard footprint 36m²
6m setback along the front

2

3

1

1 Figure 1. Courtyard house research

2 Courtyard at the rear of Vermani House

3 Private front facade of Vermani House

family bedrooms and study. They are also, unusually, where the staircase is located, which helps connect the occupants with the external conditions of light, wind and greenery in the small courtyard. This space, where the boundaries of inside and outside are blurred, is very much the heart of the house, and feels highly introverted and private, in contrast with the house front facing the street. The sole opening on this facade is the horizontal window of the master bedroom, which is set high above the floor to prevent overlooking and from which the only view is of the sky. The facade therefore turns its back to the street, underlining the importance of privacy from the outside world.

Environmentally, the insertion of an outdoor space into the middle of the house does several things: firstly, it creates pockets of shade and cool open areas, decreasing solar intensity and heat gain on walls and through openings; secondly, it increases the surface-to-volume ratio of the building, creating opportunities to ventilate through openings; lastly, it allows for the planting of trees and other vegetation, which further shade the house.

Our 2019 Wangsa House, located in an eastern suburb of Kuala Lumpur, features a large rear extension, which would have made the centre of the building gloomy and the air stagnant if not for a long, narrow courtyard that stretches deep into the interior space. Here, daylight bounces off white walls and the white gravel covering the ground, brightening the adjacent rooms, while the sculptural form of a frangipani tree allows sunlight to seep through its dispersed foliage. This outdoor space is more muted and contemplative

1 A small courtyard in the Wangsa House
2 Front facade of End-lot House
3 Roof garden of End-lot House

compared with the more extensive rear garden, which is partly paved and grassed over to provide a children's play area, recalling the hierarchies of outdoor spaces in Chermayeff's patio houses. Folding doors that open from the extensive kitchen and dining room run the length of the garden, while a long, low bench placed at the boundary between the inside and outside reinforces the relationship between the two areas by inviting occupants to sit and enjoy the outdoors. Ventilation blocks and metal mesh panels instead of glass for openings also ensure cross-ventilation throughout the day between the outdoor and internal spaces.

The private outdoor room takes a very different form in the End-lot House – a compact end-of-terrace unit initially built in the 1970s and remodelled in 2020 to suit the requirements of a young family with small children. The house is located in a busy urban neighbourhood in Kuala Lumpur and is designed to be introverted, with its street facade giving little clue of what lies behind; the only connection to the city is via the roof garden, where punched square openings provide views of the skyline above the neighbouring roofs. The space is accessed through large sliding doors from the family room, which is used to entertain friends and family, watch movies, or act as a children's playroom. These activities often spill out into the outdoor space, but the privacy of the roof garden ensures any disturbance to the neighbours is kept minimal.

Our use of outdoor rooms is encouraged by the near-constant conditions of the tropical climate, meaning occupants can enjoy it throughout the year. These rooms have also helped improve the environmental conditions of dense floor plans, increasing light levels and ventilation and allowing warm air to percolate out, as well as providing a secure and intimate space for communal domestic activities.

ENDNOTES

1 Chermayeff, Serge and Christopher Alexander, *Community and Privacy: Toward a New Architecture of Humanism*, Middlesex, UK: Penguin Books Ltd, 1966, p 214.
2 Chermayeff and Alexander, *Community and Privacy*, p 214.
3 Powers, Alan, *Serge Chermayeff: Designer, Architect, Teacher*, London, UK: RIBA Publications, 2001, pp 242–46.
4 Prip-Buus, Mogens and Jorn Utzon, *The Courtyard Houses*, logbook vol 1, Hellerup, Denmark: Edition Blondal, 2004.
5 Martin, Leslie, "The grid as generator", *Architectural Research Quarterly 4*, December 2000, pp 309–22, The article was first published in Martin, Leslie, "The Grid as Generator", in Leslie Martin and Lionel March, *Urban Space and Structures*, Cambridge, UK: Cambridge University Press, 1972, pp 6–27.
6 Martin, "The Grid as Generator", p 316.
7 Smithson, Alison and Peter, Changing the Art of Inhabitation, London, UK: Artemis Ltd, 1994.
8 Smithson, Alison and Peter, *Without Rhetoric: An Architectural Aesthetic 1955–1972*, London, UK: Latimer New Dimensions Ltd, 1973, p 8.
9 Luengo, Pedro, "Architecture in Eighteenth-Century East and Southeast Asia Chinese Quarters", *Journal of Urban History*, 0(0), 2021, https://doi.org/10.1177/00961442211029249.
10 Olgyay, Victor, *Design with Climate: Bioclimatic Approach to Architectural Regionalism*, Princeton, NJ: Princeton University Press, 1963.

Vermani House

LOCATION
Kuala Lumpur,
Malaysia

YEAR
2014

LATITUDE
3.1°N

LOCATED WITHIN ONE of the oldest suburban neighbourhoods in the heart of Kuala Lumpur, this semi-detached house was remodelled and extended in an organic design process to create additional space for its owners, a young couple with small children. Many conversations took place with the client, and later with the contractor, during the design and construction phases on how to modify the house, with details sketched out on site. One of the main issues was the form and shape of the extension, which could either be built upwards, or stretch horizontally. It was decided the addition would be better situated at the rear, hidden from public view, so that the front could remain two storeys high in keeping with the neighbourhood roofline.

A circular courtyard with terrace links the existing house with the new rectangular addition, which contains private quarters such as bedrooms, a nursery and a study. At the same time, the original part of the house was stripped bare, leaving only its external walls and reinforced concrete structure, to create an open living, kitchen and dining layout, and a large family sitting room on the upper level. These spaces are now bathed in light with large glazed openings that open onto the pool on the side of the house and the courtyard. The existing staircase was also removed, and a new one added to the

1

2

1 The courtyard terrace links the existing house with the new addition

2 House plans and section

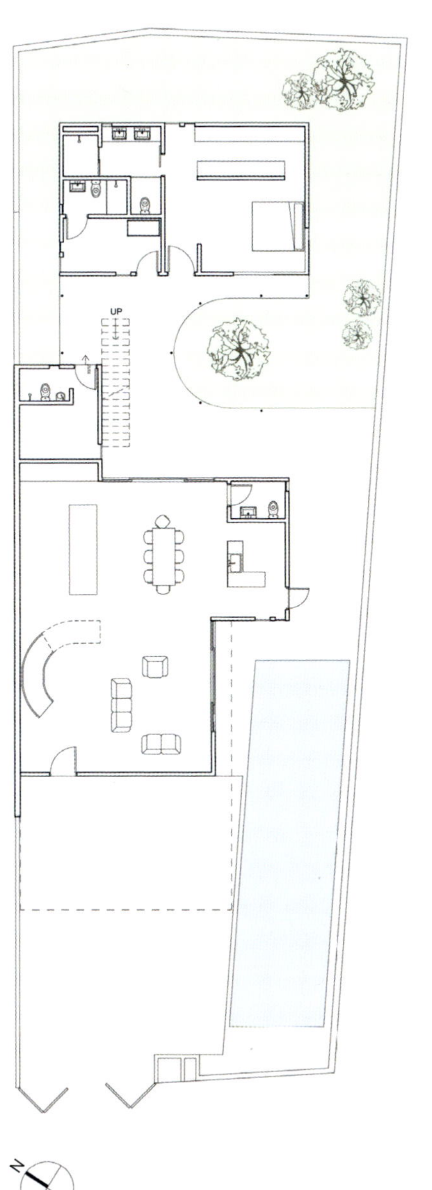
UP

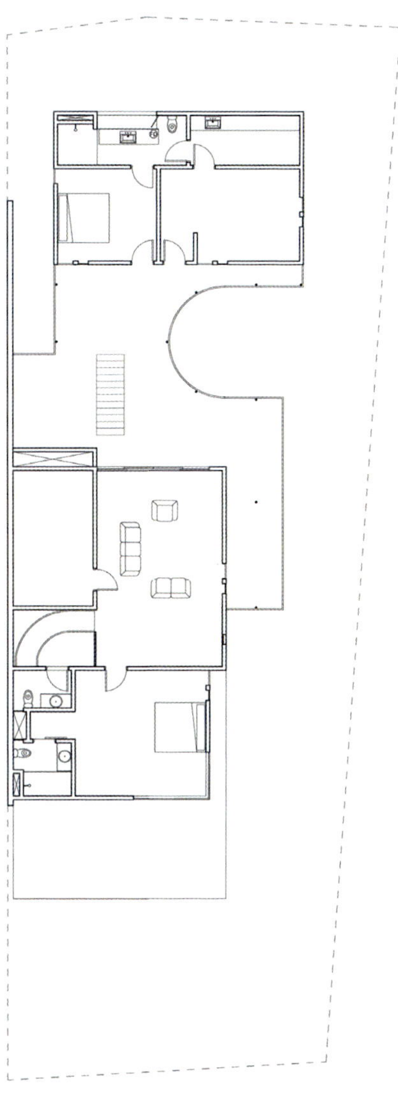

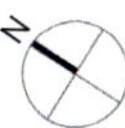
N

The guest bedroom

1
2
3

1 A metal slide occupies the old staircase space

2 Master bedroom in the new extension

3 A new staircase sits in the courtyard

courtyard terrace, while a late decision led to the installation of a metal slide in the old staircase space as a playful addition for the family's children.

From the outset, the owners agreed that the house should feel natural inside and out, and forgo the cosmetics of paint. Walls inside and out are therefore left unfinished, either as plain render or exposed brickwork, and the floors are in bare concrete, which has now smoothened from frequent cleaning and mopping. Services are also exposed, running conspicuously along surfaces in metal pipes and trays.

Wangsa House

LOCATION
Kuala Lumpur,
Malaysia

YEAR
2019

LATITUDE
3.2°N

1

2

1 The house is bright and airy
2 The new extension opens up to the rear garden

THIS IS A CONVERSION of an existing two-storey semi-detached house located in the northeast of Kuala Lumpur city. The house was in a state of disrepair and had been extended haphazardly over the years, resulting in dark and poorly ventilated labyrinth-like interiors. The conversion included a refurbishment and extension, designed to open up the house to the perimeter garden and bring in more natural light and air, removing parts of the existing internal walls and relocating the main entrance door to create a more open and fluid layout.

At the rear of the house, a rectangular volume was added at the northwest boundary to accommodate the open kitchen and dining area and create a narrow courtyard, all of which bring extra daylight and air to the centre of the house. The new space also faces the back garden, viewed through framed

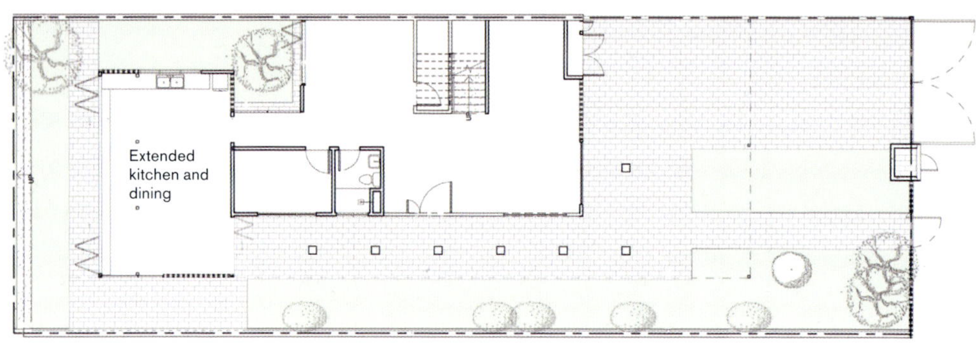

Ground floor plan

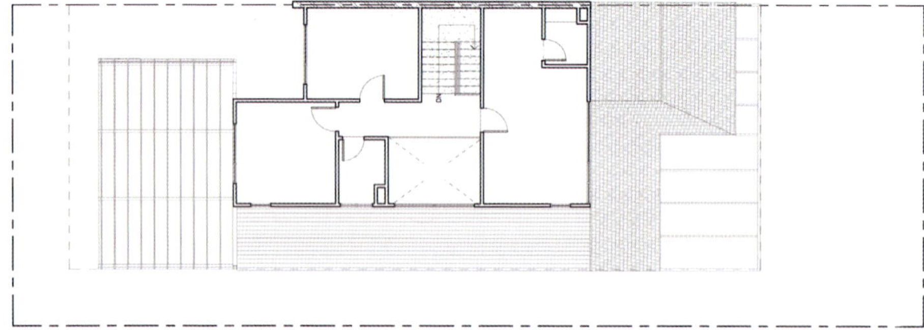

First floor plan

1 Floor plans

2 With conversions concentrated to the rear, the front facade of the semi-detached house remains relatively unchanged

3 Panels covered with steel mesh are used throughout the house

4 View out to the rear garden

mesh panels that fold open, and is lined by a stone gabion wall along the boundary. Just beyond this stone wall is a hilly terrain with fruit-bearing trees, which attract wild animals such as monkeys and squirrels, and, occasionally, wild boars. A long, low bench is placed along the wide opening facing the rear garden, enabling the occupants and visitors to sit and enjoy the greenery and its "guests". Adding the bench creates a firm boundary between inside and outside, but also encourages a connection to the external world.

Steel mesh panels and perforated concrete blocks are used generously throughout the house, resulting in bright interiors and improved room ventilation, and also create an ethereal quality as they allow refracted daylight into the internal spaces.

The new courtyard brings light and air deep into the house

27

End-lot House

LOCATION
Kuala Lumpur,
Malaysia

YEAR
2020

LATITUDE
3.1°N

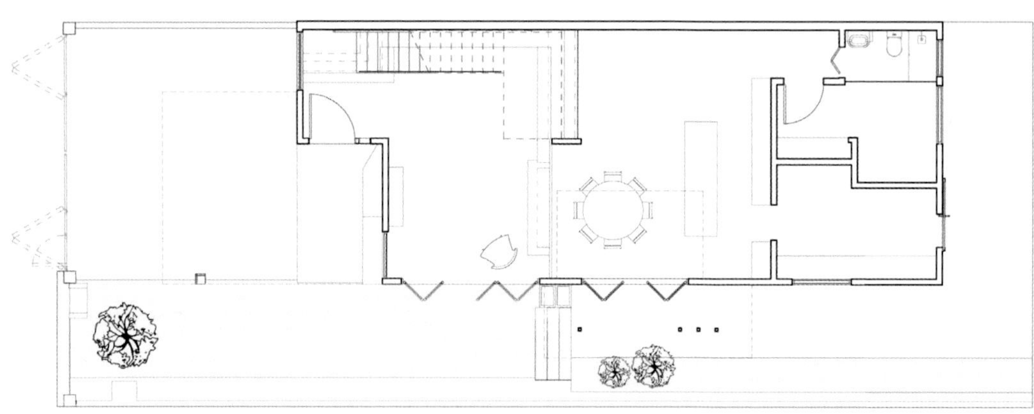

Ground floor plan

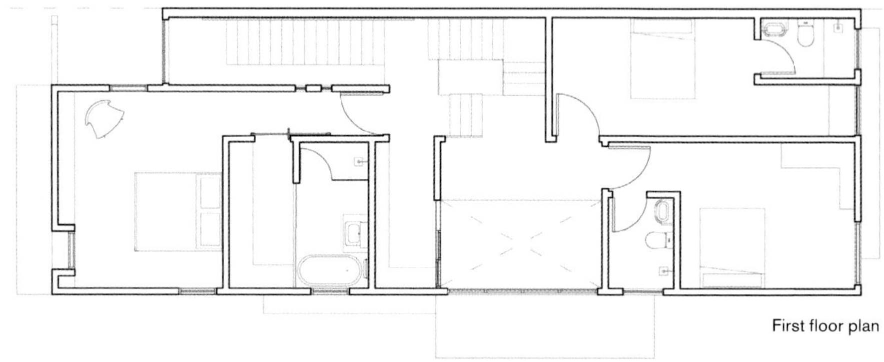

First floor plan

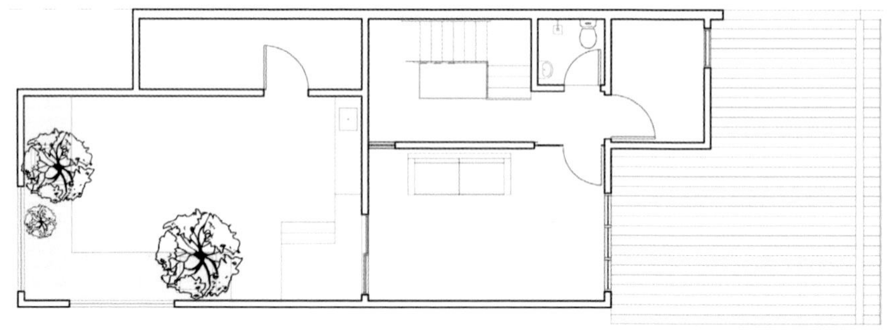

Second floor plan

1 2 3 4

1 Floor plans
2 Section
3 The ground floor is reconfigured as a single open space for daytime activities
4 The roof garden offers views of the city's skyline

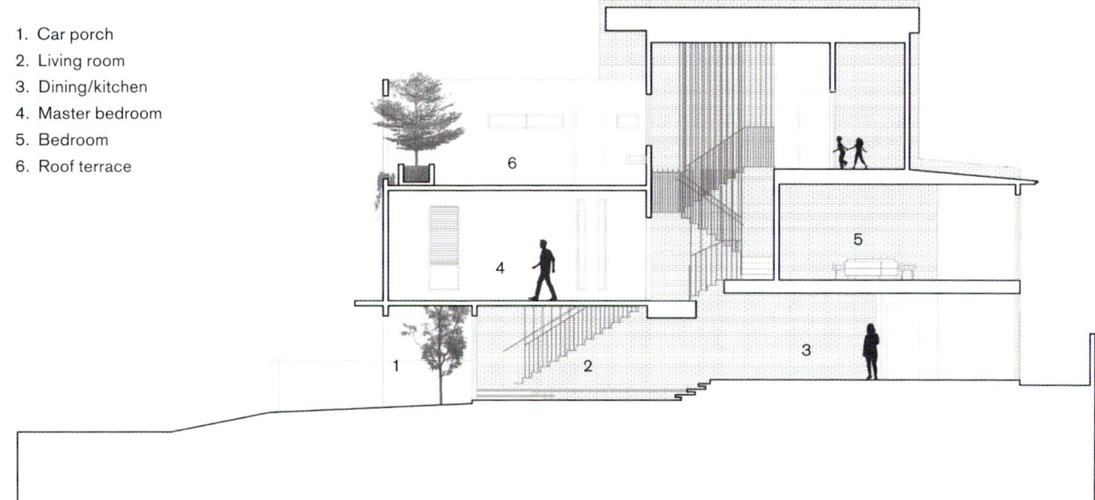

THE ORIGINAL TWO storeys of this building were constructed in the 1970s, and were split into four levels with low ceilings. Our project aimed to convert the existing structure into a comfortable family home for a couple, their two young children and visiting guests, and to provide them with an open but private house with views of the city. The conversion involved adding an extra storey at the top, which is permitted by the local authority to increase density in this part of the city, and removing non-loadbearing walls and floor slabs to create a new double-height space and staircase. This allowed the ground floor to be reconfigured as a single space for daytime activities, and for the upper floors to have larger bedrooms with good circulation in between.

The building extends along its southerly front facade with a board-marked concrete wall that hovers over the car porch. This new facade wraps around the master bedroom and then climbs upwards to enclose a roof garden at the top. Here, the concrete wall is punched with large rectangular openings that frame views onto the neighbourhood and city skyline. The tactility and rawness of the exterior are felt inside the house, where the palette is softly raw and

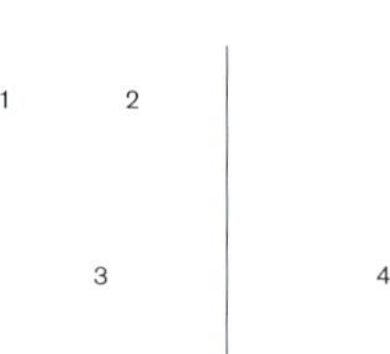

1 The dining area is a double height volume bathed in natural light

2 A tall window brings in daylight to the staircase

3 The steel staircase twists around the centre of the house

4 The staircase sits in a new location in the house

grey through the use of bricks, steel, and smooth, exposed concrete against the backdrop of white walls. On entering, one is greeted by a new staircase that extends along a brick wall and up to the top of the house, fashioned out of folded steel plates hung on steel rods. This staircase sits in a different location from the original and connects the different levels of the house in a series of flights that twists around its central core.

The split levels of the house, evident in sectional view, eliminate the previous low room heights by creating voids and removing false ceilings. In addition, the original dining room has now been replaced with a double-height volume, which, together with a new high-level window, draws light deep into the centre and creates a powerful visual connection between the ground-floor living areas and upper-floor corridors.

Connective Possibilities

Arriving at the Taj Mahal in 2019, I walked along the pathway that led to the ivory-structures with colonnaded corridors along their lengths. These corridors provide shelter and shade, and lead to other parts of the building. In one section, a small gathering of people sat on the floor in what looked like prayer. Further down, a group of women in saris and headscarves were sitting in the corridor's shadows and chatting away gaily, as people, mainly tourists, walked by. It is not known whether they live within the complex, in neighbouring areas, or even are tourists. Nevertheless, they looked totally at ease in the space, socialising and carrying on with their activities.

1 | 2

1 Buzz.ar Community Centre
2 Colonnaded corridors in the grounds of Taj Mahal complex

A "quiet" architecture with simple geometries and sheltering qualities provides space for different activities, and gives a strong identity to the place. I am reminded of the Smithsons, who once wrote about the sociological significance of public outdoor space to a community, emphasising the importance of a "socially vital life-of-the-street" where children first learn of the world outside their family.[1] The raised and generously proportioned pedestrian deck in their Golden Lane Estate housing scheme was designed to connect communities of multiple housing blocks, and to encourage chance encounters and informal exchanges, as they had witnessed from their observation of children's play and communal activities in London streets.[2] For the Smithsons, "... these pedestrian streets are not mere balconies – two women with prams can stop and talk without blocking the flow. The streets are safe play spaces – the only wheeled vehicles allowed are the tradesman's hand and electrically propelled trolleys." They therefore saw the area outside a private domain as one in its own right,

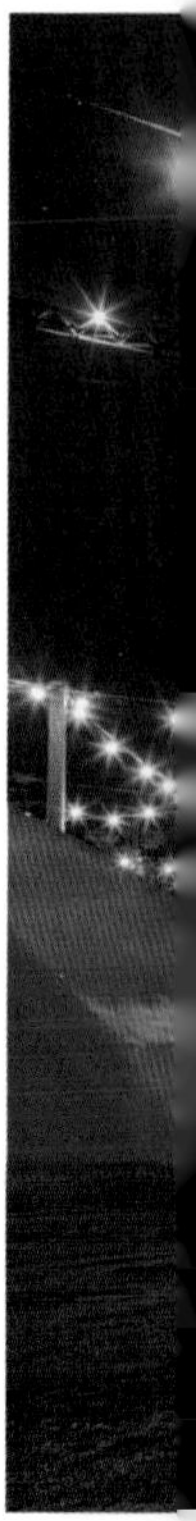

1

2 | 3

1 Pedestrian deck for Golden Lane Housing Competition in 1952 by Alison and Peter Smithson

2 Interior activities in a Malay House

3 Community event at the Buzz.ar

where residents could identify as a group and create the feeling that "you are somebody living somewhere".[3]

For space to fulfil its full potential, a certain degree of indeterminacy is required, to tempt the imagination and suggest connective possibilities the occupant may not have considered. In traditional South East Asian domestic spaces, such as the Malay House discussed earlier, and in contrast to residential spaces in the West, daily activities such as eating, sitting, working, praying and sleeping are all carried out in open interior spaces, without furniture, directly on the floor, which is often raised on stilts. Although this suggests such activities could take place anywhere in the house, on closer inspection one finds subtle changes in floor levels, the slope of the roof, the width of corridors and positioning of steps, all of which imply, rather than prescribe, possibilities for use. For example, the main space, also known as *rumah ibu* (mother's house), is set at a slightly higher level than the rest and has the tallest headroom, and is also where activities such as receiving important guests and performing prayers take place. Younger household members usually sit in the lower and narrower part of the house, while family dining happens towards the rear; but these activities can also be moved around the house, depending on need. The pureness of the internal space, and the quiet dynamics expressed by the architecture, offer adaptability while maintaining a strong sense of place and familiarity.

The traditional domestic space described above therefore offers a home one can make one's own, without alteration: simple while still referencing function, with spaces left open to interpretation. This was the approach we applied in the Buzz.ar Community Centre completed in 2019, which has hosted many activities involving small and large groups of people living in a new housing neighbourhood in Kota Kemuning, about 40 kilometres southwest

of Kuala Lumpur. Instead of anticipating changes through pre-structured and -engineered components, the building adapts to multi-occupancy patterns by emphasising planning and layout. For example, spaces and floor areas are based on carefully considered proportions and minimal expression of function. The building has a linear shape and a folded roof structure sheltering a corridor that connects an open green field and a series of enclosed cafés and shops. The corridor is 2.3 metres across, but widens at one end to become a play area with swings, and at the other, a multipurpose double-height space. The whole open area has been given the same floor finish and ceiling treatment, blurring the boundaries between the three zones.

Adaptability of space is enhanced throughout the Buzz.ar building by its open and porous character. Instead of a main entrance, multiple approaches

Above
Front view of the Buzz.ar

to the building break down hierarchy and create equality between spaces, while pathways leading to different areas, such as the adjacent car park, mall, and housing collectives, which receive high use, ensure it is well connected to the neighbourhood. However, the Buzz.ar is not a blank canvas without an identity: the building puts its tectonics and materials boldly on display, from the steel columns to its highly distinctive roof form, which folds down several times before returning to the ground at one end.

A mosque, however, is a highly prescriptive building with specific features and a finite geometry, which allow it to function as a place of daily Muslim prayer. It is also a public building closely related to the local community it serves. In our Karwa Mosque in Penang, completed in 2020, the prayer hall is a tall rectangular space angled towards Mecca. The front wall, which the

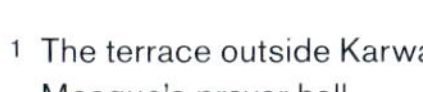

1 The terrace outside Karwa Mosque's prayer hall

2 People chatting in front of the decorative wall facing Mecca in the prayer hall of Karwa Mosque

3 Community activities taking place at the Karwa Mosque's terrace

congregation faces during prayers, is highly decorative and embellished with Islamic text and textures, while the floor is laid with carpets in contrasting colours to mark the rows and the direction the congregation should face. It is a quiet space with its use reinforced by ornamental signs.

This is in contrast to the covered terrace area just outside the prayer hall, which is raised above the busy street below, has an oval-shaped roof opening and is surrounded by a concrete bench. A double-height space, the terrace is bright and simple with very little ornamentation and is shaded by perforated screens, but it is also highly accessible with steps from street level running its entire length. Its friendliness contrasts with the formality of the prayer hall, as here visitors don't have to speak in a whisper, children can play, and it can be used throughout the day as a meeting and resting place, with mats or seats temporarily laid out for social events.

Since completion, the mosque has therefore become much more than itself and is now closely related to the life of the community. The adaptability of the terrace, which promotes social ties and a sense of ownership, makes the building as a whole an essential part of the real world and not just a hallowed space of worship.

ENDNOTES

1 Smithson, Alison and Peter, "An Urban Project", *Architects' Year Book*, no 5, 1953.

2 As influenced by the work of photographer Nigel Henderson and his partner Judith Stephen, a sociologist, both of whom were the Smithsons' friends and neighbours in Bethnal Green. Henderson took telling pictures of life on the streets that revealed elementary patterns of life created by adults socialising and children playing, Alison and Peter Smithson, *Urban Structuring: Studies of Alison and Peter Smithson*, London, UK: Studio Vista, 1967, p 14.

3 Strauven, Francis, *Aldo van Eyck: The Shape of Relativity*, Amsterdam, NL: Architectura & Natura, 1998, p 248.

The Buzz.ar

LOCATION
Kota Kemuning,
Selangor, Malaysia

YEAR
2019

LATITUDE
2.9°N

THE BUZZ.AR IS a community building created to serve a newly established neighbourhood in Kota Kemuning, about 40 kilometres southwest of Kuala Lumpur, and forms part of a large master plan that contains housing units, a park, schools and a mall. The community structure is a 1,300 square-metre building with multiple covered open spaces designed for social gatherings and events. Within it are a few small lettable units occupied by a café, hairdressers, and outlets offering pet grooming services and children's play bike and car rentals.

The Buzz.ar is physically linked to other parts of the master plan by covered walkways and landscaped footpaths in different directions, meaning that visitors can access the park, mall and housing neighbourhoods from the building, encouraging its use daily and making it a vibrant place buzzing with activity.

The building itself is linear and orientated east–west, with its main spaces facing north and opening onto an open green space and a large lake. The north side is covered by a folding roof with deep overhangs and minimal columnar support, which creates a multitude of open, shaded spaces for different activities. The folds are irregular, starting with large ones over a column-free, multi-purpose space flanked by utility areas and restrooms

1 The building faces north with a large folded roof covering

2 The building offers a multitude of open, shaded space for different activities

3 Bird's-eye view of the building

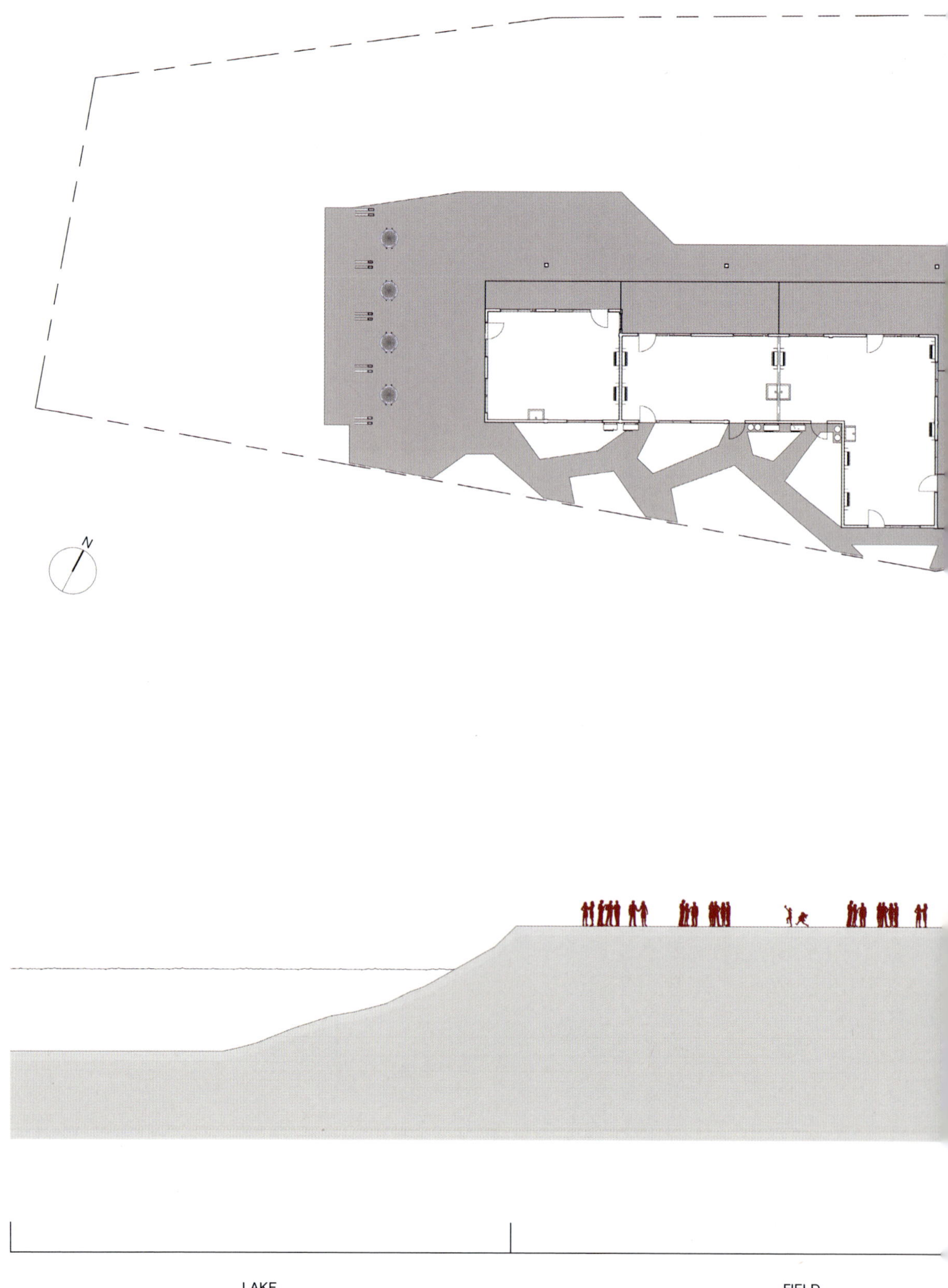
N
LAKE
FIELD

BUZZ.AR FOOTPATH SHOW HOMES

1 2

3

4

1 Play swings are hung from the structure, inviting use

2 In the bathrooms are courtyards protected by brick walls

3 The Buzz.ar Community Centre is often buzzing with different activities

4 Large overhangs cover the north terrace facing the field

along the west front. It then continues with more minor folds over the lettable units before soaring up again to shelter another open space and finally dipping into the ground. Here, play swings are hung from the structural system inviting children to interact directly with the building.

The material palette of the building is generally restrained, with painted steel, rendered brickwork, aluminium glazing and strip timber ceilings, except in the restrooms where the palette turns warmer. Here, exposed clay brick walls are used as privacy screens, and courtyards filled with a multitude of plants are inserted into the spaces to provide daylight and ventilation.

The geometry of the roof can be seen replicated throughout the building: in the glazing configurations, tall windows are broken up by angular framed panels; the floor finish combines three different pebbled textures laid in a geometrical pattern; and in the multi-purpose space, a backdrop wall is composed of three-dimensional angular blocks from floor to ceiling painted in different shades of grey.

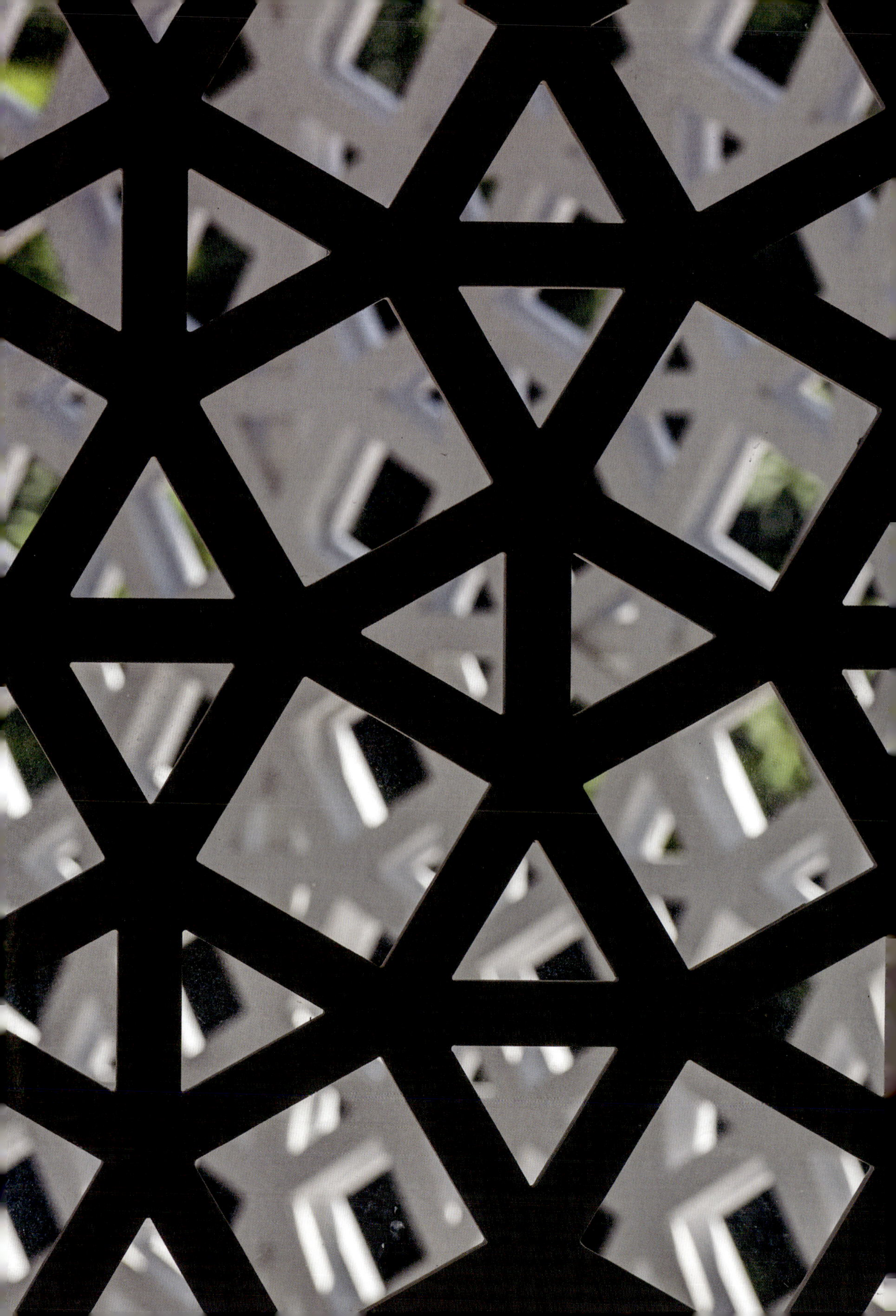

Karwa Mosque

LOCATION
Penang, Malaysia

YEAR
2020

LATITUDE
5.5°N

THE KARWA MOSQUE has served the local Muslim community living in Tanjong Tokong, Penang, Malaysia, since 1897. This area was once a quiet fishing village, until the 1970s, when urbanisation and densification started to take over. The most dramatic transformation was the creation of a new extended coastline to allow the building of large malls and high-rise apartment blocks, leaving only a small portion of the original village standing.

The planning of a new mosque began in late 2014, and aimed to replace the old timber and concrete structure that had been extended and remodelled haphazardly over the years. The new building sits on the tight corner of a bustling road intersection surrounded by mainly tall buildings, a position that allows it to act as an informal gateway to the existing village to its north-east.

1 2 3

1 The mosque acts as a gateway to the existing village

2 Karwa Mosque sits on a raised plinth at a busy road intersection

3 The terrace is a large shaded space with a courtyard

1 Terrace
2 Minaret
3 Female ablution
4 Office
5 Female WC
6 Main prayer hall
7 Male ablution
8 Mosque mortuary room
9 Male WC
10 Mimbar
11 Imam room
12 Bilal room

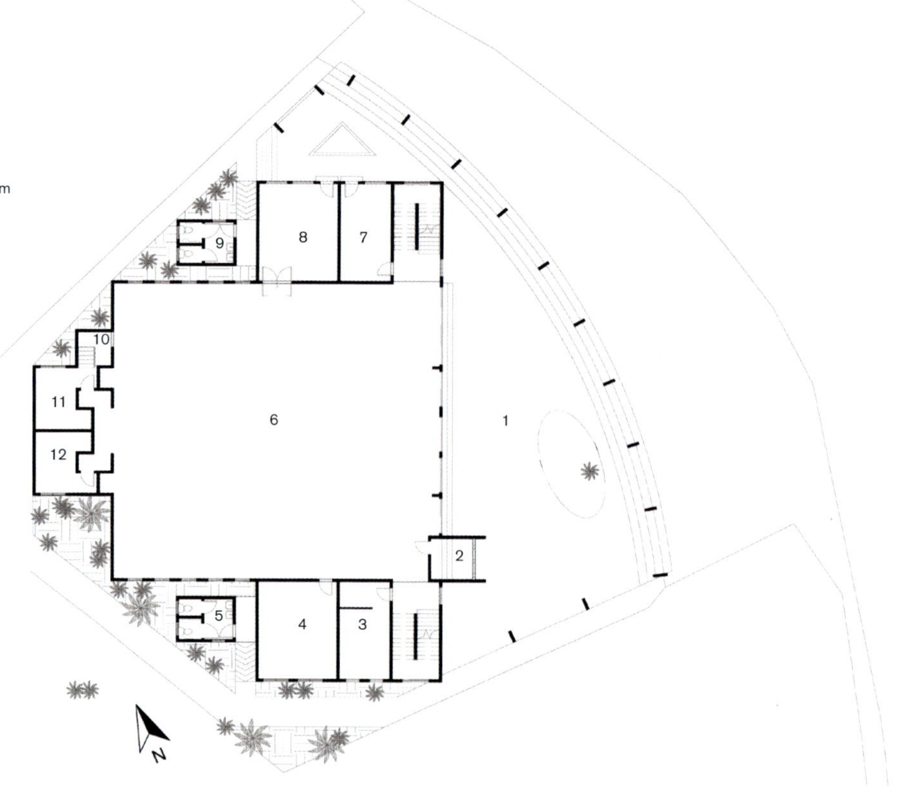

1 Terrace
6 Main prayer hall
10 Mimbar
11 Imam room
13 First floor prayer hall

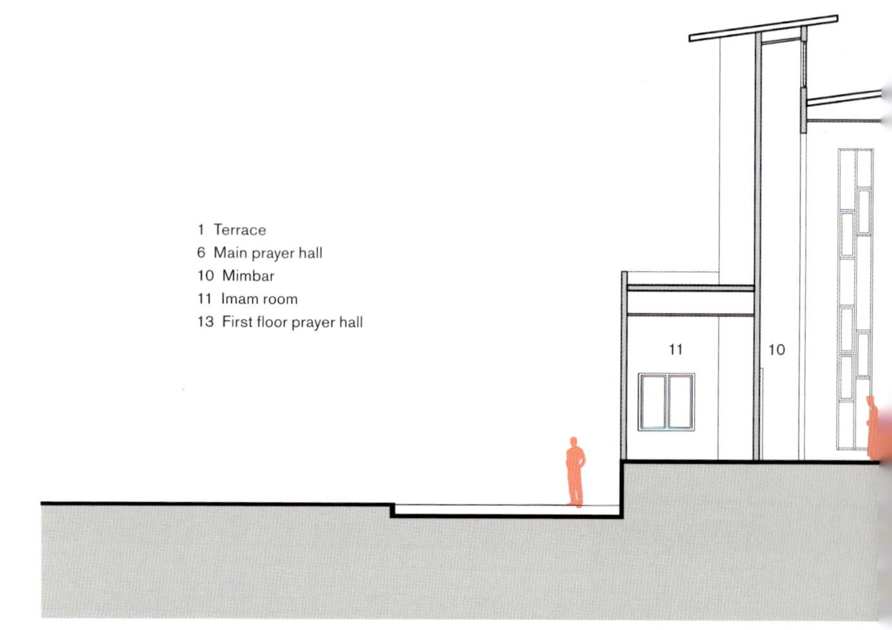

1

2

1 Floor plan
2 Section

New mosques in Malaysia tend to be bold expressions of symbolic identity, involving domes, arches and dynamic arabesques. The Karwa Mosque avoids this, instead favouring subtle expressions of simple patterns and forms rooted in Islam, and expressing its identity in a series of perforated panels of Islamic motifs arranged in a curve that corresponds to the edge of the road. Beyond this facade, a minaret looms tall and is covered with the same decorative panels. The mosque is painted white, a nod to the array of colonial structures found all over Penang.

The Mosque sits raised on a plinth above road level and is reached via a series of steps placed between evenly spaced columns. Beyond these steps is a large, shaded terrace with a landscaped courtyard, similar to the verandas seen in local vernacular domestic architecture. This terrace is used by the local community for gatherings and events and as a spill-out space during crowded Friday prayers. Most days, young children can be found playing there while waiting for their parents to complete their religious observances.

The courtyard terrace leads to the main prayer hall. This is a large double-height space with a square plan oriented towards *qibla* or Mecca. The *mihrab* wall, where the congregation faces, is decorative in a subtle and quiet way, and is split into three recessed sections covered with green-coloured glass panels and appliquéd religious texts. The walls between the recesses are lined from top to bottom with carved perforated panels, punctuated by a *mimbar* opening where the *imam* stands to deliver sermons. The whole decorated *mihrab* sits bathed in bright natural light that streams in from the tall windows in the walls on either side.

Supporting spaces such as meeting and study rooms, offices, restrooms, and ablution and nursing rooms are situated alongside the prayer hall, while a mezzanine level is attached to the rear of the hall to accommodate the increased number of people during Friday and Eid prayers.

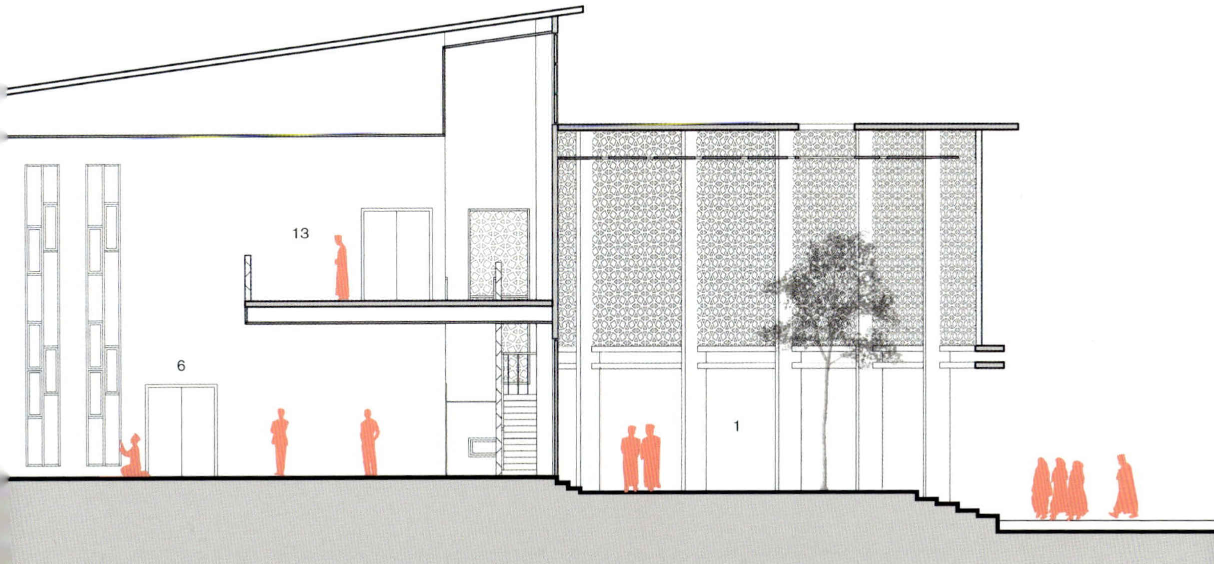

BIOGRAPHIES

Eleena Jamil

Eleena Jamil is a Malaysian architect born in Penang. She graduated from the Welsh School of Architecture, Cardiff University, in the UK. She joined the Cardiff architecture faculty as a teaching assistant while completing her MPhil and PhD postgraduate research. Her PhD thesis, titled *Rethinking Modernism: The Sugden House and the Mother's House*, examined the idea of "ordinariness" and "vernacular imagery" as an alternative to the reductive limitations of modern architecture. Eleena set up her eponymous architectural practice in Kuala Lumpur in 2005 and focuses on developing buildings within the context of Malaysia and South East Asia. Her work has been founded on research into each brief's specific social and climatic imperatives within a broader cultural framework. She was shortlisted for Dezeen Architect of the Year 2018 and featured in *100 Women: Architects in Practice*, published by RIBA in 2023. She has lectured widely and was recently appointed Adjunct Professor at the National University of Malaysia (Universiti Kebangsaan Malaysia).

Dean Hawkes

Dean Hawkes is an architect and teacher. He is emeritus professor of architectural design at the Welsh School of Architecture, Cardiff University, and an emeritus fellow of Darwin College, University of Cambridge. He taught and researched at Cambridge from 1965 to 1995, where he was director of the Martin Centre for Architectural and Urban Studies from 1979 to 1987, before returning there after his retirement in 2002 as a fellow of Darwin College. In 1995, he was appointed professor of architectural design at Cardiff. He has also held visiting professorships at schools of architecture in Hong Kong, Singapore, Glasgow, Huddersfield and Leicester. His research is in the field of environmental design in architecture; publications include *The Environmental Tradition* (1996), *The Environmental Imagination* (first published 2008; second edition 2020), *Architecture and Climate* (2012) and *The Architect and the Academy* (2022). His buildings, in partnership with Stephen Greenberg, won four RIBA architecture awards, and in 2010, he received the RIBA Annie Spink Award in recognition of his significant contribution to architectural education.

ACKNOWLEDGEMENTS AND SPECIAL THANKS

I would like to express my deepest gratitude to Dean Hawkes, who tutored me in the fifth year of architectural studies and supervised my MPhil and PhD research dissertations at the Welsh School of Architecture, Cardiff University. His writings, research and design work hugely impacted my development as a practising architect, and I would like to thank him for writing a foreword for this book.

I sincerely thank the fantastic project team at Artifice Press, especially Publishing Director Anna Danby and book designer Richard Seymour – and special thanks to Davina Thackara, who edited the text.

I want to thank my family, my husband, Aziz Marzuki, and my children, Aleya, Adam and Ayesha. I am forever grateful for their limitless support.

Projects featured in this book would not come to fruition without the commitment and creative contribution of the architects, designers and collaborators who have worked alongside me. I thank them for their contributions.

Office members present and past

Yow Pei San, Lina Izzati Muhammad, Bahirah Rahman, Ishak Sukran, Anise Kaz Ahmad Kamal, Cheah Zhi Bin, Dalia Qistina Nasaruddin, Nur Izzati Narozi, Yusri Amri Yussoff, Nurhidayah Ab Razak, Nurnajdah Najib, Barbara Chang Huey Yi, Amos Tan Chi Yi, Dzaleha Mohd Khairi, Noor Lydia Sabrina Noor Zilan, Dyone Tham Chui Wei, Nur Azreen Mohd Ramli, Zamrina Embong, Sufiah Muhadzir, Mohd Shahril Ramli, Arif Zakwan Abdul Hamid, Nur Amalina Hanapi, Rashida Rashid, Reham Alwakil, Olwyn Roche, Rameeja Mohd Hussain, Rudi Hakimi Mohd Nasrumi, Mohd Nur Husaini Jailani, Muhammad Haziq Rosli, Hariani Md Yunus, Muhamad Fathi Mustafa, Anis Fatini Murhan, Farhatun Nada Sulaimi, Ervena Ela Suzeana Mohamed Affandi, Norhasliza Mohamad, Nurhasnadira Hashim.

Collaborators

Dr Veronica Ng, Mohamed Rizal Mohamed, Sateerah Hassan, Mohd Adib Ramli and Azim Sulaiman (SABD Taylor's University)
Shalini Ganendra (Shalini Ganendra Fine Art Gallery)
Carmelo Ignaccolo and Anastasia Ignatova (UN-Habitat for WUF09 Pavilion)
Ir Ahmad Mazlan Othman (Bamboo Jungle Adventures)
Mohd Ramadhan Abdul Hamid
Tham Teck Hai (TH Tham Engineering Sdn Bhd)
Dr Lynn-Sayers McHattie and Marian McAra (Glasgow School of Art)
Elena Tamosiunaite (British Council UK)
Florence Lambert, Erica Choong and Syarifah Said (British Council Malaysia)

Image credits

Book cover: The Garden Library by GarisPXL

Unless otherwise stated, all drawings, model views and photographs of projects are courtesy of Eleena Jamil Architects. The following credits apply to all images for which separate acknowledgement is due.

Alvar Aalto Foundation p 11 (figure 1)
David Yeow Photography pp 2–3, pp 125–27, pp 130–31, p 132, p 140 (figure 2), p 141, pp 158–65
Diane Durongpisitkul pp 60–61
GarisPXL pp 16–19, pp 91–97
Nurhidayah Ab Razak p 20 (figures 1 & 2), p 23 (figure 4), p 76 (figure 1)
Insular Life Assurance Co p 65 (figure 5), p 88 (figure 1)
Lin Ho Photography p 140 (figure 1), pp 151–57,
Marc Tey Photography p 26 (figure 1), p 72, pp 74–75, p 77 (figure 3), pp 128–29, p 139, pp 142–49, p 172, p 182–83, pp 188–89
Pixelaw Photography p 21 (figure 3), p 23 (figure 3), p 28, p 31, pp 32–33, p 35, p 37, p 38 (figure 1), p 39 (figure 3), pp 40–43, pp 52–59, p 70, p 73, p 166, pp 169–71, pp 175–77, pp 180–81
Rupajiwa p 106, pp 116–23
Root Photography p 22 (figure 2)
Shutterspeak p 26 (figure 2), p 27, p 65 (figures 1 & 2), p 66, pp 79–81
TWJPTO pp 184–185
With permission from The Harvard Library p 168 (figure 1)
Alamy p 11 (figure 2)
Shutterstock p 12 (figure 2)

This book is published by Artifice Press Limited, a company registered in England and Wales with company number 11182108. Artifice Press Limited is an imprint within the SJH Group.

Artifice Press Limited
The Maple Building
39–51 Highgate Road
London NW5 1RT
United Kingdom

+44 (0)20 8371 4047
office@artificeonline.com
www.artificeonline.com

Designed by Richard Seymour
Written by Eleena Jamil
Printed in Spain by Grafo

ISBN 978-1-911339-51-9

British Library in Cataloguing Data. A CIP record for this book is available from the British Library.